101 Things to Do 'til the Revolution

Ideas and resources for self-liberation, monkey wrenching and preparedness

by Claire Wolfe

Loompanics Unlimited
Port Townsend, Washington

This book is sold for information purposes only. Neither the author nor the publisher will be held accountable for the use or misuse of the information contained in this book.

101 Things to Do 'til the Revolultion

Published by:
Loompanics Unlimited
PO Box 1197
Port Townsend, WA 98368
Loompanics Unlimited is a division of Loompanics Enterprises, Inc.

Cover design by J.R. Williams
Color by Mary Fleener

ISBN 1-55950-157-X
Library of Congress Card Catalog 96-78459

Contents

Dedication

This book is based on the premise that, when governments turn bad, the best people ultimately become criminals. The people don't change; the laws do. Initiative, dissent, individual pleasures, and exercise of one's basic rights become "crimes." Obscure regulations and technical paperwork violations are used to destroy people who dare to speak their minds.

The ideal citizen of a tyrannical state is the man or woman who bows in silent obedience in exchange for the status of a well-cared-for herd animal. Thinking people become the tyrant's greatest enemies.

Before their thunder roars, there is a period of anticipation, in which more occurs than the literal-minded tyrant can ever understand. A few overt acts of sedition shatter the heavy peace. But the greater force, unrecognized, rolls forward in near silence, as millions of individuals quietly withdraw their consent from the state. The pundits call it apathy. They could not be more wrong.

That time is now and we are those people.

This book is dedicated to you, the Enemy of the State.

Acknowledgments:

Many thanks to Kevin Burt, who added great ideas and humor to this project. Thanks to Charles Curley, who read the manuscript, contributed his "Bureaucracy Encounter Form", and above all put up with me through my writer's deadline frenzy. Thanks also to attorney William Curley for the use of his business card, to Marshall Fritz for quotes about the government education system, to Delbert Gilbow for his discussion of *mala prohibita* and to the many organizations and authors I've cited in this book.

Foreword

America is at that awkward stage.

It's too late to work within the system, but too early to shoot the bastards.

On the road to tyranny, we've gone so far that polite political action is about as useless as a miniskirt in a convent. But most people are still standing around numb and confused, knowing something's wrong with the country, but hoping it isn't quite as bad as they're beginning to suspect it is. Only a few folks with really cranky tempers or unusual foresight are ready to throw off their chains.

Something's eventually going to happen. Government will bloat until it chokes us to death, or one more tyrannical power grab will turn out to be one too many. Maybe it'll be a national ID card (or datachip), maybe random, roving wiretaps on our telephones. Maybe it'll be one more round of "reasonable gun control" or one more episode of burning children to death to save them from "child abuse." Whatever. Something will snap. The time will come, and we'll all know it. People will force change — maybe from the barrel of a gun.

The "revolution" of the book title may never be a shooting war. I hope to hell it isn't. But it will be a time of explosive change, of chaos, of entrenched power fighting for its life against the forces of freedom, or of power collapsing and leaving a vacuum. It will happen.

Until then, what do you do?

What do you do if you care about freedom? What do you do if you don't want to be an apathetic toad, a mad bomber, or a Good Little Citizen begging an unhearing congresscritter to give back the rights he and his buddies swiped from you? ("Dear Congressman Bacon: You're such a busy and important person, I'm sure this little matter has just slipped your mind temporarily. But 90 percent of the federal government is unconstitutional. Since I know how much you value your oath to defend the Constitution, I'm sure you'll want to abolish all the unauthorized agencies and programs right away. Please don't forget to repeal all the illegal laws and get rid of taxes while you're at it. Thank you in advance for taking care of this matter. Yours truly, Goodie Twoshoes.")

> *For government consists in nothing else but so controlling subjects that they shall neither be able to, nor have cause to do [it] harm...*
> — Niccolò Machiavelli

Well, here are 101 things you could try.

The ideas in this book mostly fall into three categories:

- Self-liberation — things that are a good idea no matter what the government does or doesn't do;
- Monkey-wrenching — little irritants to help wake people up and bring the system down(bit by bit);

- Preparation — things that could help you survive the worst of the mess, once the government's fecal matter does finally hit the rotary airfoil.

Some are high-profile. Some are low-profile. Some are for people who find creativity and challenge in confrontation. More are for those of us who'd just as soon avoid fuss. Because different things work for different people, some of these items are even contradictory. That's one of the beauties of a free society.

Wherever needed, I've added a little bit of how-to information or a phone number, address or reference book so you can learn more on your own.

So pick and choose among all the items here, or let them inspire you to come up with your own.

Obligatory legal notice

One final warning. There are a few ideas in this book that would probably be illegal if you actually carried them out. A couple more might be illegal in one state but OK in another. There are even some that, while perfectly, absolutely legal, might still get you arrested by some cop who's learned that intimidation is the only "law" that's necessary when dealing with sheep. Merely standing up for your rights these days can be a dangerous thing.

I can't — and wouldn't — advise you to do anything illegal. Of course, these days, there are 11 million pages of federal laws and regulations (which would take you your entire lifetime to read). There are 200 pages of new laws and regs every day. There are God knows how many state and local laws, and there are 250 million scared, cowed citizens, who have no idea what's legal or illegal anymore — leaving them prepared to follow any order issued by someone with a badge or a federal ID card. If I advised you to fill a mud puddle in your driveway, chances are I'd be inciting you to violate the federal wetlands act. If I suggested you kill a cockroach, we'd probably both be conspiring to violate the Cockroach Protection Act of 1973. On the other hand, if you didn't kill that cockroach, you'd probably be violating the Urban Sanitation Act of 1967.[1]

We're reaching the Orwellian point at which "that which is not forbidden is compulsory."

But the most illegal thing of all is the U.S. federal government, which, in every day, in every way, violates the highest law of the land, the Constitution and Bill of Rights. So what the hell? The worst thing you could do doesn't even begin to compare to that.

In order to keep from getting arrested or sued, however, the publisher and I have to tell you that any ideas about illegal or potentially illegal ideas are *For Educational Purposes Only,* and that we aren't recommending that you follow any of them.

Well, that's true. I'm not advising or recommending that you do anything. Advice is your mother's job. Let your own mind, heart and conscience be your guide to life. The only thing I hope is that you live in freedom, as you see fit, with as little interference as possible from government busybodies and bullies. If any of the suggestions in this book help you do that, good, but your life belongs to you. Live it well. Live it bravely. Live it smart.

Oh, okay, just *one* teeny bit of advice: please don't shoot the bastards. You know how touchy governments can be about such things, and what nasty forms their tantrums take. So please, please, please, no violence — yet.

---

[1] Both these acts are figments of my imagination, of course. However, thousands of other acts are figments of Congress's imagination. Scary, isn't it?

It is just as difficult and dangerous to try to free a people that wants to remain servile as it is to enslave a people that wants to remain free.
— Niccolò Machiavelli

Note: This book is written from a libertarian/free-market perspective. It presumes a commitment to: gun rights, drug legalization, free minds, free markets, the elimination of taxes, the abolition of federal police agencies, and the least possible amount of government — maybe no government at all. If you fall elsewhere in the philosophical spectrum, you probably won't like some of the ideas here (though I hope you'll keep an open mind). In any case, feel free to adapt the techniques to your own positions. Have fun.

Chapter One and Only

1. Don't write to your congresscritter

Put down that pen! Close that word processing program! Forget all that happy crap you learned in civics class about sharing your views with your "representative." You don't have a representative any more. You merely have someone who thinks he or she is your "leader," unfettered by either your opinions or the Constitution.

Your congresscritter assumes the role of the overseer in the field. You are merely the "n-word" toiling under super-vision. The benevolent massa wants sincerely to "help" you, as long as you toil and obey.

Marx was wrong: religion isn't the opiate of the masses; in modern America, the drug that keeps us numb, dumb and well-behaved is a belief that we can still make a difference by politely voicing our views to our would-be rulers and owners.

The fact is, every minute you spend writing to your congressperson is a minute you don't spend on useful freedom activity. Every minute you spend writing to your congressperson is a minute you fool yourself into believing you're accomplishing something when you're not.

What happens to your letter

Here's what happens when you write your congresscritter. Your letter is carried into his or her office in a big plastic crate along with thousands of other letters. An aide scans it to see what it's about and sticks a form letter in the mail to you. Then the aide enters your name in the computer, with a notation that you wrote to say, "Vote yes on X" or "Vote no on Y."

If you're lucky, they might actually get the topic right. If you're *really* lucky, they'll record you as being on the side of the issue you're actually on. They're just as likely to record you as being one of your own political enemies, though. Doesn't that make you feel special?

Even if you get what appears to be a "customized" reply, it was written by an aide and probably signed by a machine. The congressperson never saw either your letter or his or her own reply.

If you send an e-mail, an automated system scans your message and zaps back a reply, without your message having been seen by human eyes.

The whole process is designed to say, "There, there now, little citizen, your congressperson cares" — when, in fact, nobody cares.

If you're rich, famous, powerful or influential (or if they think you're a dangerous loony, but that's not an impression you want to make), you have a chance of being heard by someone in Congress. Otherwise, the only time you have the slightest chance of influencing a congressperson's views is when your letter — or fax or phone call — is one of several thousand expressing the same opinion. Then it's only going to help if: 1) the congressperson is already on your side of the issue and wants to wave a basketful of supporting letters during a floor debate; or, 2) the congressperson's seat is insecure and he or she *has* to do what the people want for a change, or else.

The only method that might do a bit of good

If you just can't live without writing to your congressperson, keep a stack of pre-addressed postcards handy, and when you're so roused up about something you simply have to do it, write, "Vote no on HB2000, the Counterterrorism Act sponsored by Rep. Bigbro," or "Vote yes on SB504, the Privacy Amendment sponsored by Sen. Rarebird."

Bright-colored postcards get more notice, just as shiny objects best attract the attention of mindless rats.

Keep it that simple. Don't waste your time on reasoned argument or constitutional issues. Use those arguments elsewhere, with people who might actually listen.

> *In order to become the master, the politician poses as the servant.*
> — Charles de Gaulle

2. Govern yourself

Have you ever daydreamed, "If I were king...?" Well, you are. You are the only legitimate ruler of the Nation of You. Do the job well — and have fun.

3. Love the ones you're with

Are you in a miserable relationship? Do you and your significant other rub each other raw? Do you fight about the same things all the time without resolving anything? Or do you just quietly endure each other's presence without truly communicating or caring?

Then get the hell out!

Freedom begins at home. You can't have an honest hope of freeing the country if you can't free yourself first. Besides that, when the bad time comes — as it inevitably will — you'll either need to be completely independent or have supportive people around you.

The same thing is true of all your relationships. If your parents control you by guilt, criticism or handouts-with-strings-attached, detach yourself. If you hate your boss and can't resolve the problem, figure out what job you can *realistically* do better — and go.

You've got to support your children. That's an obligation you hung around your own neck when you brought them into the world. But beyond that, nobody has a claim on you except those claims you assent to — and you can withdraw your assent any time you want to.

> *"For your own good" is a persuasive argument that will eventually make a man agree to his own destruction.*
> — Janet Frame, writer

4. Don't vote; it only encourages them

If voting could change the system, it would be illegal. That's old, but wise, advice from an anarchist.

In some of the world's worst dictatorships, voting is *compulsory*. Think about the implications of *that*.

> *Philosophy of government: From each according to his ability; to each according to his irresponsibility.*
> — Claire Wolfe (With no apologies to Marx)

5. Do write letters to newspapers and magazines.

While congresspeople don't listen, real people still do. As more and more people begin to realize something is dreadfully wrong, more will be willing to consider different ideas. Take all those reasoned arguments you used to use on your congresscritter and send them into the world via newspapers, magazines, guest editorial columns, posters, speeches — or by whatever means works best for you.

If you're fortunate enough to live in a small city or rural area where the local paper prints every letter it receives, write sparingly. Otherwise readers who disagree will begin to tune you out: "Oh, it's just Pat Jones again."

And here's a "monkey-wrench" variation on this honorable activity:

Persuade the village idiot to write really gross letters to the editor supporting your opponents' positions. You could also fake such letters yourself. Cite obviously bogus "facts." Overstate or deliberately misstate the positions of the organization you claim to be supporting. You could make these letters ironic and humorous, but you'll have more luck getting them printed and have more chance of making your opponents look bad if you make them look serious. For instance:

> "Dear Editor: I agree with the National Education Association. At its annual convention in Chicago last month, the NEA passed a resolution that parents who home school their children or use private schools should pay a 15 percent federal income tax surcharge. As one NEA member commented, 'Since these people are responsible for the collapsing school infrastructure, it's only fair that they should pay for the privilege of abandoning the public school system.' I think the NEA's proposed surcharge is a good start, but more needs to be done. The next step should be to outlaw all

home and private schooling. After all, if the government doesn't control what children learn, we could end up with a country where people learn things they shouldn't know and believe anything they want."

"Dear Editor: The Partnership for a Drug-Free America is right. Everybody who uses marijuana should be thrown in jail for the rest of their lives! Anybody who has more than an ounce of it should be executed! Nothing else has worked, so it's time to get really tough in the War on Drugs. It's time to show those sick, evil, perverted marijuana addicts the government means business."

"Dear Editor: I absolutely agree with Handgun Control, Inc. The government should take all guns away from everybody. Start with gang members, but next, take the guns away from all those hunters. All they do is kill pretty animals. It's also a well-documented fact that 85 percent of all hunters are wife-beaters; at least 575,000 hunters shoot their wives to death every year. We don't need people like that in America."

6. Write poetry

Poetry? Write poetry?!! Sure. It's good for the soul. Besides that, since no one takes it seriously, it's a good place to express all your most subversive thoughts. You're less likely to attract trouble than if you go around writing manifestos, yet you're a lot more likely to get quoted and remembered.

Okay, if poetry is too effete for you, add music and call it a song.

7. Question authority

Never presume anyone is right — or has more rights than you do — just because he or she is standing in front of a classroom, wearing a uniform, talking legalese, shouting from a pulpit, appearing in the media or carrying a government ID card.

Ask questions. Demand answers. Make 'em show you their facts. If some newspaper prints a poll that "proves" something the media would just love to be true, don't believe it unless you've seen the raw data for yourself and verified that the polling methodology is legitimate. If someone claims to be an expert, find out how expert they really are. If a bureaucrat or official claims to have a right to do something (or make you do something), politely ask which law authorizes it — then check for yourself.

Be polite at first. But never settle for anything less than a straight, provable answer.

Our educations and social training have usually taught us to accept authoritative statements at face value. We learned knee-jerk belief at out mother's knee and our first-grade desk. We also learned we'd get in big-time trouble by doing otherwise. So unless we have specific reason to doubt, we tend to believe. We must reverse that!

If you haven't seen it, smelled it, touched it, tasted it, experienced it, proved it for yourself, assume it ain't so. (That goes for everything you read here, too, of course.)

Yes, this can be a hassle, and as often as not, you'll be treated like a jerk for questioning authority. So be polite but firm. Or, if you don't want to go through the hassle of confrontation or the time and trouble of checking data, just make sure to keep the questions in your heart.

Once you stop fearing government, the government fears you.
— Robert D. Graham, tax rebel

8. Kill your TV

Go ahead. Take your television out to the shooting range or the nearest plinking site and have yourself a ball blasting its big old Cyclops eye and blowing out its little silicon brains.

What, you say you like TV? You can use it in moderation? You're careful to distinguish between good entertainment and blatant propaganda and other trash?

Not likely. When we're watching TV, our brain waves are nearly identical to what they are when we're hypnotized. Think about it — the way a TV set draws your eyes even when you're not particularly interested in what's on the set... the way your eyes seem to glaze over and feel as if they're rolling back in your head as soon as they focus on the screen. That's hypnosis, people.

That means information, impressions and assumptions get fed directly into your unconscious without your conscious mind being fully able to edit and sort them. The effect is the same whether you're watching *Masterpiece Theatre* or *Married, with Children*. No matter how aware you are in general, and no matter how alert you believe yourself to be while watching TV, no matter how critical you think you are of the material you're watching, at some level, someone else is controlling your mind. Is that how you want to live?

While TV contains many poisonous messages, those specific messages aren't the worst problem. Marshall McLuhan was right. With TV, the *medium is the message* ...and its message is that you are nothing but a passive blob, fit only for sucking up what someone else wants you to see, hear, believe and know.

I often hear politically aware people saying they need to watch TV to keep an eye on what the mainstream media are saying and doing. Not true. You can get more accurate news from non-mainstream sources, and you can get a full shot of mainstream information from the Sunday paper — a medium which leaves you in control of your faculties even when its content is as bullshit-filled as that of the TV.

I'm tempted to call TV a drug. But the vast majority of drug users can control their drug use. Millions of people use drugs without screwing up their brains and drugs don't come with pre-programmed messages; you take 'em, then you choose, through your own actions and inclinations, what messages to let in. TV's effects are more insidious than any drug ever known to mankind.

An independent mind is critical to living free. So drop that electronic seducer off a cliff. Try that new box of cartridges out on it. Run over it with your lawn tractor. Bury it in your backyard. Free yourself from mind control and time control.

Then use all that newly free time and consciousness to LIVE.

P.S. If you absolutely can't tear yourself away from that cathode ray tube, watch some good videos. *Braveheart* is a terrific one for starters.

9. Get rid of your dependencies

Picture this. Your favorite vice is taken away from you. Bang! It's gone! No more booze, cigarettes, coke, cola or whatever. Now what do you do?

There's nothing wrong with drugs, cigarettes or anything else you like to do and can do without harming others, but there's *everything* wrong with being dependent.

You could lose access to your favorite vices in an economic collapse, a natural disaster, a guerrilla war, or if you end up in jail. If you're a slave to your habits you can easily become a slave to anyone who can control your habits — anyone who dangles the desired thing in front of you and tells you you can have it if you just cooperate. Even if you don't end up in that dire circumstance, you could still spend a lot of time in pain and struggle over the loss of something that really should never have been so important.

Free yourself. Now. Don't get caught unawares. Enjoy the things you enjoy — fine! But be absolutely certain that you're in charge of them, not vice versa.

Don't forget — media blather to the contrary, chemicals and unhealthy habits aren't the only thing people let themselves become dependent on. You could be just as "hooked" on books, computer games, model ship building, work — or a whole bunch of other things—as some people are on alcohol or heroin. Examine your heart. If you find any "can't live withouts" there (other than the basic human needs for food, water, warmth, etc.), start practicing doing without them right away.

Freeing yourself from petty dependencies can also be good training for freeing yourself from big dependencies — like dependence on government.

10. Be ready to profit from others' dependencies

In event of an economic collapse, nationwide trucker's strike, revolution, or other emergency, there are going to be a lot of people, less smart than you, who haven't rid themselves of their private slaveries.

At that moment, he or she who holds a tidy store of pint-sized booze bottles, cigarettes, chocolate bars and other goodies could do well. It's cynical. I personally wouldn't do it, but I also don't think dependent people deserve much sympathy; they'll simply be living with the consequences of their own choices.

(Please don't use this kind of secret stash as a substitute for cleaning up your own act. There's no guarantee your stash of goodies will remain secure, and you simply don't ever want to risk getting caught weak and whimpering.)

Every society honors its live conformists and its dead troublemakers.
— Mignon McLaughlin, writer

11. Just say NO

Here's some advice found on the back of the business card of attorney William Curley of Gillette, Wyoming:

If the police officer says...
"Please open the trunk."
"May I come in the house?"
"I'd like you to do some tests."
"Do you understand your rights?"
"Would you like to give a statement?"

Then politely, on the advice of counsel....

Just say NO.

The difference between a democracy and a dictatorship is that in a democracy you vote first and take orders later; in a dictatorship you don't have to waste your time voting.
— Charles Bukowski

12. Know the difference between *mala in se* and *mala prohibita.*

Mala in se translates to "bad in and of itself." Murder, rape, robbery, child molestation and similar acts that harm others are *mala in se.* These are the things that nearly all people at all times, have considered wrong.

Mala prohibita translates to "bad because it's forbidden." Smoking marijuana, not getting a building permit, having consensual sex with an unapproved partner, and filling in the wrong ditch on your property are *mala prohibita.* They're only "wrong" because some piece of paper says they are, or because some scary people may hurt you if you do them.

What makes the government any more capable of deciding right and wrong than you are? Nothing, that's what. Well, nothing except raw power — which has never been a useful guide to ethics or morality.

Knowing the difference between *mala in se* and *mala prohibita* can help guide your behavior toward your fellow humans when there's no outside authority left to guide you, or when "authority" has become so corrupt and laws have become so numerous and nebulous that there are no longer any sensible legal principles worth obeying. (We're about there now.) At that point, only acts that are *mala in se* should be off limits.

When things really get bad, you may have to judge for yourself whether blowing up an IRS office or shooting a fedgoon is *mala in se* or *mala prohibita.* Harming those who harm others, committing violence against those who do violence can be good in itself, when done at the right moment, in the right way. You really have to be sure: Half-cocked action on a half-baked idea isn't good enough.

No one is bound to obey an unconstitutional law and no courts are bound to enforce it.
    −16 Am. Jur., Sec. 177 late 2d, Sec. 256

13. Use pre-paid phone cards for privacy

When you use one of those pre-paid phone cards, available at shopping malls, discount stores and convenience stores, no record of the call goes on your phone bill, even if you place the call from your living room. A police agency or freelance snoop who gets hold of your bill won't learn anything.

A notation of your call *does* go on the records of the card vendor. So don't think of this as a completely fail-safe method, but it can protect your privacy against casual snooping or police fishing expeditions.

If you bought the card using cash or a money order, there's also no paper trail linking the card to you. So a call 1) using a cash-purchased card and 2) placed from a phone booth could never be traced to you, even by the most diligent search methods.

The state calls its own violence law, but that of the individual, crime.
    — Max Stirner

14. Join a gun-rights group

In my humble opinion, the two things free people must preserve *at all costs* are privacy and gun rights. Because even if we lose everything else, we can use these to win our other lost rights back. On the other hand, if we are disarmed and if the government can track every move we make, every purchase we make, every trip we take, they've got us.

So fight, fight, fight for these rights. Here are three of the best groups who can help you keep your gun rights.

S.A.F.E. (Second Amendment is for Everyone)
10412 N. Eighth Avenue, #3
Phoenix, Arizona 85021
(602) 375-0060
e-mail: safe@indirect.com
Web site: http://www.indirect.com/www/safe
   SAFE is a smart and defiant bunch of libertarians who make a point of standing up for their rights, even when it means defying arrest to do so. Their position is: "NO COMPROMISE; the only way is to remain armed & SAFE." Operating mainly in Arizona so far, they teach others by example how to insist on, and win back, rights the government unlawfully steals.

Jews for the Preservation of Firearms Ownership
2872 Wentworth Avenue
Milwaukee, Wisconsin 53207
(414) 769-0760
e-mail: jfpo@prn-bbs.org
Web site: http://www.msc.net/~lpyleprn/jpfo.html
   JPFO is a civil rights group. They take the position that gun control is a precursor to genocide, and that our own Gun Control Act of 1968 was translated (in some places word-for-word) from a Nazi law Senator Thomas Dodd brought back from Nuremberg after World War II. They, too, take a NO COMPROMISE position. They are a tax-deductible education group; no lobbying. You don't have to be Jewish to join or support JPFO.

Gun Owners of America
8001 Forbes Place, Suite 102
Springfield, Virginia 22151
(703) 321-8585
e-mail: crfields@gunowners.org

Web site: http://www.gunowners.org

GOA lobbies congress (and gets listened to more than you as an individual can). They also help defend people whose rights have been abused by federal or local law enforcement agencies. They, too, are a NO COMPROMISE gun group, watching out for every sneaky piece of wording in a bill, every quiet little committee vote a congresscritter makes.

Forget the NRA. They're the biggest and oldest and they've certainly done some good over the years, but they are absolutely committed to compromise — even when they could win instead. They recently co-wrote a Pennsylvania state gun-control law (Act 17, passed late in 1995) with Handgun Control, Inc. then lied about the bill's anti-gun provisions. They talk very, very tough, but they'll sell you down the river while bragging about all the good they're doing you. Put your money and your hopes elsewhere.

So we drove down the road, and I was lookin' for a house that looked like if there was somebody at home that it'd be somebody that didn't carry a gun or didn't have no weapons in the house, so they couldn't use them.

—An Arkansas 17-year old, pleading guilty to multiple counts of burglary, theft, aggravated robbery and rape

15. Be a Simon Jester

Simon Jester never existed. He was merely a character in Robert Heinlein's delightful science fiction novel, *The Moon is a Harsh Mistress*. In fact, Simon didn't even "exist" in the novel; he was a fiction invented by other fictional characters to irritate the government and spur rebellion.

"Simon" popped up now and then to plant anti-government poems, cartoons and sayings on the scene, then fade mysteriously away.

Don't you think there could be a little "Simon Jester" in us all? Wouldn't it be a delight if, all across the land, evidence of Simon's presence appeared to remind would-be rulers they are neither sacred nor safe — and to let our fellow freedom lovers know they are not alone?

Here's how

Have some stickers printed up with thought-provoking sayings. (It's easy if you have a computer; just buy some Avery labels at the stationery store and print the stickers on your printer.) All you need to do is make sure your printer will handle the sticky labels. If it won't, print yours at the local Kinko's or equivalent.

Carry a sheet of them and slap them everywhere you go: phone booths, rest room stalls, newspaper vending machines, park benches, post office or school bulletin boards, store windows — wherever they'll be noticed.

Short, sharp and/or funny sayings are best. Try these:

Taxes: the politicians' way of saying, "Pluck you!"

America was neither founded, nor freed, by the well-behaved.

Our forefathers should have fought for representation without taxation.

God created men and women: Samuel Colt made them equal.

Isn't it about time we found Congress in contempt of The People?

I don't trust a government I can't shoot back at.

When only cops have guns, it's called a police state.

BATF: Bad Attitude Toward Freedom.

If laws worked, there would be no crime.

Work harder: millions on welfare are depending on you.

Support the Chinese Underground: buy an SKS and bury it.

My country, yes. My government, no.

Writing to Washington won't help; he's dead!

Four boxes keep us free: ballot, jury, soap and cartridge.

Orwell is starting to look like an optimist!

Freedom-fighting women don't have hot flashes; we have power surges.

You cannot strengthen the weak by weakening the strong. — A. Lincoln

Horiuchi: "Drop that baby or I'll shoot!"

If we all ignore the government, it'll go away.

I am not a number. I am a free man. — The Prisoner

Where is John Galt now that we need him?

FBI: Freedom Bashers, Inc.

A little revolution... is a good thing. — Thomas Jefferson

Defend America against the government.

Rebellion against tyrants is obedience to God. — Thomas Jefferson

Armed women = polite men.

If the government were in charge of sex, we'd be extinct.

Washington is a joke. Have you laughed lately?

Never trust anyone with a loaded government.

The government is not your daddy.

The government is not your mommy.

Keep your laws off my body.

Freedom is the ability to say, "I won't!"

I'm from the government. I'm here to help you. BLAM!!!

Big Brother is here — and he's retarded!

Buy a gun. You'll need it.

Yesterday it was David Koresh. Tomorrow it could be you.

Fear of government is the second step to wisdom.

Support your local heretic.

To permit is to control.

Don't drink to excess. You might shoot at tax collectors and miss. — Robert A. Heinlein

Government: get out of my bed and my pocketbook.

I resigned. I will not be pushed, filed, indexed, briefed, debriefed or numbered. My life is my own.
— The Prisoner (Patrick McGoohan)

16. Don't be a terrorist

Terrorism is properly defined as organized, systematic violence carried out against *non-government* targets for the purpose of producing fear and submission. Despite all the blather in the media and on the floor of Congress, an act has to have all those elements to be true terrorism.

Therefore, people who attack *only government employees and property* aren't terrorists. They're guerrilla fighters. Whether they are fighting in a good cause or not is up to history — and each of us individuals — to judge. But terrorists they ain't.

---

*When even one American — who has done nothing
wrong — is forced by fear to shut his mind and close
his mouth, then all Americans are in peril.*
—Harry Truman

17. Oppose property seizure with all your might

I said earlier I thought gun rights and privacy were the two
things we needed to fight hardest to preserve. But there's one
other battle — one we're presently losing big time — that
could be the make-or-break issue between tyranny and
freedom in America. It's civil forfeiture.

First, some background:

In the early days of the War on the Bill of Rights...er, I
mean, the War on Drugs... Congress passed a law allowing
cops to confiscate the assets of suspected drug dealers
without criminal charges or criminal trials. The rationale
given to the public was that cops *needed* to seize their fancy
boats, cars, planes and money to keep drug dealers from
fleeing the country.

Thus began a nationwide program of taking money and
other possessions from people without due process. Wealthy
drug dealers were hardly the people targeted. Then and now,
the typical seizure victim is a relatively poor black or
Hispanic person who can't afford to go through the expensive
civil process to "prove" him or herself "innocent" of a crime
he or she wasn't even charged with.

(It gets worse. In federal seizure cases, at least, the
forfeiture victim has to post a bond of several thousand
dollars merely to gain the right to contest the case in court.
Until he or she does, no judge will even look at the case to
determine whether the seizure is legal. That's kind of tough
to do when they've taken everything you own. Once in court,
the victim, now impoverished, isn't usually even entitled to a

court-appointed attorney because it's a civil, not criminal, case. In one case, the DEA claimed the victim wasn't impoverished — based on the value of the person's car — *which the DEA had seized and was in the process of selling!*)

In 1990, the U.S. Justice Department issued a memo to law enforcement agencies across the country urging them to use civil forfeiture as a means of raising money.

At that point, the process escalated into a kind of government-sanctioned protection racket. What the Mafia can't do, cops are *encouraged* to do and they are doing it with a literal vengeance.

Occasionally in the early 90s, federal courts issued very limited, wishy washy edicts against forfeiture. In one case, they said cops couldn't take real estate without a hearing because bad guys couldn't use real estate as a means of escape from justice. In another, they said cops couldn't confiscate property then bring criminal charges in the same case because that would be double jeopardy — the forbidden act of punishing the same person twice for the same crime.

However, cops at federal, state and local levels never stopped. Civil forfeitures went dramatically up, not down.

Civil forfeiture is based on a medieval concept that inanimate objects — like houses and cars — can be guilty of wrongdoing. In other words, the cops claim they aren't punishing *you* if they take your car or your house; they're punishing the *thing*. Never mind that they know it's a lie. Today cases with crazy names like *United States v. $405,089.23*, *United States v. 9844 South Titan Court*, and *United States v. Real Property Located at Incline Village* are common.

From bad to worse — punishing the innocent

Then in early 1996, the Supreme Court issued the Bennis decision and things got even worse: A lot worse.

Tina Bennis was a poor housewife from Michigan. She and her husband had bought a beat up van for $600, which she needed to take their children to school and doctor appointments. A few weeks later, local police found her husband having sex with a prostitute in the van. They confiscated the van and sold it, keeping all the proceeds. But in doing so, they punished not only the "guilty" husband (if you accept that the free-market transaction of trading money for sex is a crime), but his wife, who didn't even know what her husband was doing.

Stefan Herpel, an Ann Arbor lawyer concerned about civil forfeiture, took Mrs. Bennis' case and fought it all the way to the Supreme Court, giving up most of his other legal practice to fight what he perceived as the most inexcusable and dangerous injustice threatening the country today. It looked like the perfect case for defending the rights of an innocent person denied due process.

But the Supreme Court said no. They said cops can take *any* piece of property that's *ever* been connected to any sort of crime, even if the owner had nothing to do with it, even if the owner didn't even know about it. One justice said he didn't particularly like the idea, but that they couldn't find anything in the Constitution to prevent it.

The members of the Supreme Court are obviously unfamiliar with the Fourth Amendment ("The right of the people to be secure in their persons, houses, papers, and effects against unreasonable searches and seizures shall not be violated...."), Fifth Amendment ("No person shall...be deprived of life, liberty or property without due process of law; nor shall private property be taken for public use without just compensation."), and the Fourteenth Amendment ("....Nor shall any State deprive any person of life, liberty or property, without due process of law....").

Odd, isn't it, that the alleged arbiters of constitutionality couldn't find, in months of deliberation, what you or I could show them in five minutes?

Be that as it may, the situation is now this:

If a friend borrows your car and is found with an open bottle of beer in it, your car may be history. If your cousin sells a stolen boom box from your back porch, your house is history. If your neighbor plants marijuana on an isolated corner of your farm, kiss your farm and your livelihood good-bye.

That nation is desirable in which wealth and friends can really be enjoyed, not the one where wealth can easily be taken away, and where friends in time of necessity abandon you...
— Niccolò Machiavelli

Now, theoretically, this also means that, if a passenger on a luxury cruise ship has an assignation with a prostitute in his cabin, the cops can seize the cruise ship. It means that if a petty thief employed by General Motors hides stolen goods on company property, the law can seize and sell the whole manufacturing plant. Or (as one editorial cartoonist graphically suggested) if a janitor is caught smoking a joint in a bathroom of the Supreme Court building, the Supreme Court building could be confiscated and sold.

It isn't going to happen quite that way, of course. The government class will be exempted by its privileged status and the government grafters will leave most of the wealthy and powerful alone — because they have the resources to fight back.

No, it's you and I who are in danger here, and not only if our friends or relatives commit crimes without our knowledge. Simply if some government goon decides to target us.

Talk about things going from bad to worse! As if the Bennis decision weren't outrageous enough, on June 24, 1996, the Supreme Court, in its infinite wisdom, declared, "We hold that these... civil forfeitures are neither punishment nor criminal for purposes of the double jeopardy clause." So don't feel bad when they take your house and bank account, friends. You haven't been punished. You've just, out of the goodness of your heart, made a "contribution" to your friendly U.S. or neighborhood government.

The court passed judgment on two separate forfeiture cases June 24; both involved seizure of assets from drug users. One decision was unanimous; the other was 8 to 1. Freedom doesn't have *any* friends on the U.S. Supreme Court. So take care of your own backside, people, because the Injustice System isn't going to do it for you.

If you have a nice car, boat or house whose sale could enrich the coffers of some cop agency, look out. If you have a valuable collection of anything, beware. If you express unpopular political opinions — well, you're probably toast.

All it takes is for one sly cop, offended by your vocal opposition to drug laws (for instance) to plant one joint on your property and your house and land are *gone*.

All it takes is for one officious "social welfare" bureaucrat to allege child abuse, true or false, and you can lose everything.

All it takes is for cops to learn you've downloaded a "dirty picture" from an Internet site, and you can wave bye bye to your computer — and maybe to everything else you own.

Don't imagine I'm exaggerating. It doesn't even have to be a real crime. In several states, they're already doing it for misdemeanors. In some southern jurisdictions, cops routinely stop drivers who fit a made-up "drug dealer" profile, search them and their cars, confiscate every dime the person is carrying, then turn them loose — no charges, no evidence of any crime. In California, they're talking about confiscating cars from those terrible threats to society — car owners who fail to renew their license tags!

This is serious shit, people. Now that the government has proved forfeiture can be used to intimidate minorities without the media or the general public getting huffy, watch for forfeiture to be used as a tactic to silence *all* forms of opposition.

That's exactly why we've got to oppose this loud and clear. Because this is the dividing line between tyranny and the America of our ideals. If they get away with this, we become the cowed victims of a police state, terrified to speak up, terrified of what our friends and family members might accidentally inflict on us, unable ever to be certain we own our own property — chattel-victims of the state.

What to do about it
First, some legitimate, mainstream stuff:

Join FEAR — Forfeiture Endangers American Rights
P.O. Box 15421
Washington, DC 20003
voice: 202-546-4301
1-888-FEAR-001 (if you can't afford the toll call, please)
e-mail: paff@net-lynx.com
Web site: http://www.fear.org

This is a small, underfunded organization, but it's fighting as hard as it can. It works with lawyers, publishes information about the status of various seizure cases, and maintains an Internet Web site with detailed information on some particularly outrageous cases. FEAR could use your money and help — and you might need FEAR's help someday, too.

Read *Forfeiting Our Property Rights* by Congressman Henry Hyde. Though he's not our friend in a lot of other ways, Hyde is one of the few members of Congress actively defending our rights to due process. While the legislation he's introduced is incredibly wimpy, his background information on the issue is good.

If you are a victim of forfeiture or an attorney, read *Forfeiture and Double Jeopardy: How to Turn Prosecutorial Overreaching into Release of Prisoners or Return of Seized Property* by FEAR's Brenda Grantland. For more general information, try Grantland's *Your House is Under Arrest*.

These books are available from FEAR. By the way, the absurd case names I mentioned above are real; information on these and others and can be found on FEAR's Web site.

For a guerrilla tactic

Well, let's call this one a fantasy or a hypothetical situation, since actually doing it would be illegal...

Bury some drugs in the garden of a local judge or city council member who thinks forfeiture is a great old thing. Then call an anonymous tip line and say you saw them doing it one moonlit night as you were passing by. Let them experience first hand just how "wonderful" forfeiture is.

Or you could scatter some "drug paraphernalia" and marijuana seeds under the seat of the mayor's teenage son's car. Then call that hot line.

Put the right chemicals into an unlocked shed on the back of a local drug enforcer's lot and — *voilà* — you have a meth lab to report. (Loompanics even has books to help you choose the appropriate chemicals.)

Of course, it might be hard to get a politically connected person arrested, and even if he or she does get busted, the cops aren't as likely to steal a politician's home or car as yours, but keep trying. It's even possible that, if the particular politician has political enemies, they'd *love* to engineer an arrest and property seizure.

Even if the tactic doesn't result in seizure of a bigshot politician's property, you might have some fun watching Mr. or Ms. Holier-Than-Thou squirm and deny.

If forfeiture results, of course, it's perfect justice. After all, under the Bennis decision, the Supreme Court says it doesn't matter *who* actually commits the crime. So what if it's really *your* crime committed on the mayor's property? The highest court in the land, our August Masters in Washington, say the mayor's house is guilty — and deserves what it gets!

Somethin's happening here, and you don't know what it is — do you, Mr. Jones?
— Bob Dylan

18. Celebrate the Fourth of July

Instead of sending Christmas cards, have some Fourth of July cards printed up. Include a pithy quote about freedom. Something from the founding fathers would be nice, or maybe one of the other quotes scattered around this book.

19. Celebrate April 19

On April 19, 1775, the farmers and villagers of Lexington and Concord stood against the might of the British army and set us on the road to independence.

On April 19, 1943, small bands of desperate Jews in the Warsaw ghetto, armed with a few dozen firearms and little experience in their use, decided to fight rather than submit to the Nazis' "final solution." They held off SS troops for weeks before they were defeated.

On April 19, 1993, the United States government sent tanks against members of an unapproved religion. More than 80 people died from fire or poisonous gas, including two dozen children, for the alleged crime of failing to pay federal taxes on some firearms.

On April 19, 1995, someone bombed the Alfred P. Murrah Federal Building in Oklahoma City. Was it was an angry ex-soldier and his friends, as the government claims? Or was it the government itself in a successful attempt to pass "counterterrorism" legislation? Whichever view you adopt, the bombing was a sign of the growing distrust between free Americans and the government caste.

In Massachusetts, April 19 is still celebrated as Patriots Day in memory of the stand at Concord and Lexington. Unfortunately, that state's government has long forgotten the issues and significance of the thing it pretends to celebrate.

But you need not. April 19 is a day worth noting for many reasons. A good day for:

- Sending cards
- Writing letters to the editor
- Holding rallies
- Writing guest editorials
- Conducting memorial celebrations
- Reminding your anti-gun Jewish friends that armed defense is part of their history and religious teachings
- Renewing your own resolve never to give up or give in
- Simply remembering

People — pardon me, journalists and politicians— have often accused me of believing that I'm above the law. And yet, who isn't? Everywhere you prod it, even with the shortest stick, the established system isn't simply corrupt, it's unequivocally putrescent. The law is created by demonstrable criminals, enforced by demonstrable criminals, interpreted by demonstrable criminals, all for demonstrably criminal purposes. Of course I'm above the law. And so are you.

— L. Neil Smith, *Pallas*

20. Cultivate some Mormon friends

There is a really bad joke that goes like this:

"Do you know what's in the most basic disaster survival kit?"

"A rifle and a directory of the local Mormon ward."

I apologize to my Mormon friends, but the truth behind the joke is that Mormons, also called Latter-Day Saints, are among the best people on earth when it comes to disaster preparedness.

Don't go shooting them. They'll shoot back and you'll deserve it. You may want to learn from them before disaster strikes. Many Mormons, as required by church doctrine, live a life of preparedness, canning, drying and storing food, laying in emergency heat, light and cooking sources, and otherwise planning to prevail over catastrophes. Stockpiling a years' supply of food (or more) is part of their doctrine and their daily lives.

Mormons run a number of fine survival stores in Utah and other western states. Some are listed in *Some places to find all of the above,* No. 83. Your local ward or stake may also have a buying club that would enable you to purchase bulk goods at a better rate than you could get elsewhere. (They may not let a "gentile" join. If so, perhaps a Mormon friend could make purchases for you.)

If you're interested, ask a Mormon acquaintance or look in the phone book under Church of Jesus Christ of Latter-Day Saints.

Whether you agree with their teachings or not, the Saints have other valuable lessons to teach us all. They are one of the most cohesive social groups in the world. Their church-run welfare system — based on the dignity of work, voluntary contributions and mutual aid — is more effective and more truly humane than any government system ever devised.

I am not a number. I am a free man.

— The Prisoner (Patrick McGoohan) Also known as "Number Six"

21. Don't give your Social Security number

Everybody wants your Social Security number. Your car insurer requests it. So does your health insurance company. Some phone companies do. Go to school? They'll ask for your number. Open a checking account, give a number. Sign up for a paging service; they want the number. Drivers license? Not without a number. Apply for credit? Give a number, please.

Less than a month ago, I even had to fight to keep a county *library* from demanding my number before giving me a flipping *library card*! (They said they needed it for their collection agency in case I stole a book!)

Although these people all act as if they're entitled to your number, in most cases, they aren't. You have the right to keep your number from them — and you should.

Since you're reading this book, you probably have some idea why it matters. In case you're one of the millions who spouts your number without thinking every time somebody pushes your Social Security button, here's the reason: Privacy.

The more that number is used to identify you, the more the feds, the state, or any talented computer hacker can find out about you. Where you live. What you own. What medicines you take. How much you pay in taxes (or whether you pay). They can access your education records, employment records, mental health treatment records, criminal history — you name it. Your whereabouts can easily be tracked by finding out where you work, where your house is, where you make credit card purchases and so on.

Everyone who asks for your Social Security number will assure you that their particular databases are absolutely confidential and secure. The person telling you that may even believe it. But if *you* believe it, I have some nice swamp land in Florida to sell you.

When the Roosevelt administration was trying to sell its Social Security Ponzi (pyramid) scheme to the public in the 1930s, they assured everyone that *absolutely, positively*, the Social Security number would *never* be used for any purpose but record-keeping within the Social Security system itself.

I am old enough that my card says right on it "NOT TO BE USED FOR IDENTIFICATION." Yours may not. They dropped that in embarrassment after the number had long been allowed to become, by default, a national and all-purpose ID number. It's so convenient for "them." So dangerous for us.

It doesn't have to be that way. There are steps you can take. Every one of these steps carries some risk — from the risk of having people think you're a jerk to the risk of federal persecution. But, again, if we want to regain our independence, risk is something we must accept. Which risks — and what level of risk — only you can determine for yourself.

Things to do about it

1. You can, if you truly detest being part of this system, rescind your Social Security number and do without one. If you decide to take that course, write to the Social Security Administration at the following address:

Social Security Administration
Office of Public Inquiries
Attn: Attempts to Withdraw
Mail Stop: 4-H-8 Annex
6401 Security Boulevard
Baltimore, Maryland 21235

"Attempts to withdraw" is the administration's own phrase. You might prefer to change it to "Attn: Withdrawals." You have as much right to withdraw as a slave does to be free.

Taking this course, however, targets you as "one 'a them right-wing, hate-mongering, freemen, constitutionalist nutcases" and will land you immediately in another database — that of suspected terrorists and revolutionaries. And guess what? That database will contain your Social Security number, too.

So on this course of action, let's post a notice: "Secretary of Health and Human Services Warning: Social Security is 'good' for you. Attempts to withdraw from the system may be hazardous to your health."

After rescinding your number, you can take up a constitutionalist fight to keep your job, open savings accounts, or whatever, without a number. Sovereign citizen groups can sell you "substitute W8 and W9 forms" along with instructions on filling them out; these are forms filed by people claiming not to be U.S government citizens. (See *Consider sovereign citizenship*, No. 63.) It's exhausting, but some people seem to thrive on the confrontation.

2. You can tear up your card and refuse to be identified that way ever again, but trying to live in the modern world after doing so is darned near impossible.

3. You can lie about your number. The fine for doing so is only $50, and I've never heard of anyone actually having to pay it. But it's frightening how easily lenders, schools and government agencies will detect a false number and demand a real one. If you do make up a number, you must be careful to choose a "realistic" one. Social Security numbers have a pattern. For instance, the first three numbers are a code representing the state where your card was issued. The second two denote the year of your birth. If you pick a number that says you're 36 years old when you're actually 21, someone might notice. The book *Understanding U.S. Identity Documents* (by John Q. Newman, Loompanics Unlimited, 1991) gives a chart showing the actual codes used.

4. If you want to erase your past and start over, you can get "genuine" new ID documents, including a Social Security number, from the government using one of the methods detailed in books like *Understanding U.S. Identity Documents*. But this is risky; the feds might have caught on to last year's surefire method of obtaining false documents, and clampdowns allegedly aimed at illegal immigrants are causing tighter controls on all of us every day. Also, if you freely give your new Social Security number to all those private and public bureaucrats, you simply begin creating a new data trail for yourself. If your intent is to escape the past,

false documents could help. If, on the other hand, your intent is to have privacy in the present, a new Social Security number alone won't do it.

5. Finally, you can keep that number but learn when to stand on your legal rights and refuse to reveal it. Believe it or not, Congress once actually passed a law to protect your rights, rather than violate them. On the next two pages is some information about it from a group called the Heritage Caucus. The following is *not* copyrighted, and the caucus encourages you to make copies and give them to anyone who unlawfully requests your number. (I have edited their text to remove redundancies and correct grammatical glitches; all claims, quotes and case citations are theirs.)

As with everything else in this book (and the world), you should verify the accuracy of this information for yourself. However, I've found that merely pulling a copy out of my wallet and waving it in front of a bureaucrat's face usually does the trick, with no further discussion or proof necessary.

PRIVACY ACT LIMITATIONS ON SOCIAL SECURITY NUMBER USAGE

Since many people objected to extensive loss of privacy which accompanied the use of computers, Washington responded by passing the "Privacy Act," Title 5 of the United States Code Annotated 552(a). It states quite simply that, "It shall be unlawful...to deny any individual any right, benefit or privilege provided by law because of such individual's refusal to disclose his Social Security number." Due to it, courts have ruled, in part:

"Right of privacy is a personal right designed to protect persons from unwanted disclosure of personal information..." (*CNA Financial Corporation v. Local 743*, D.C., Ill., 1981, 515F, Supp. 942, Ill.)

The District Court in Delaware held that the Privacy Act:

"Was enacted for [the] purpose of curtailing the expanding use of Social Security numbers...and to eliminate the threat to individual privacy and confidentiality posed by common numerical identifiers." (*Doyle v. Wilson*, D.C., Del., 1982, 529G, Supp. 1343.)

In the strongly worded *Guideline and Regulations for Maintenance of Privacy and Protection of Records on Individuals* it is stated:

"(a) It shall be unlawful...to deny to any individual any right, benefit or privilege provided by law because of such individual's refusal to disclose his Social Security account number."

The Privacy Act calls for the following penalty for knowingly violating it:

"(A) Actual damages sustained by the individual as a result of the refusal or failure, but in no case shall a person entitled to recovery receive less than the sum of $1,000; and (B) the costs of the action together with reasonable attorney fees as determined by the court."

It is suggested that you take someone with you when you assert your rights under the Privacy Act. He or she will witness the incident and testify (if necessary) to the facts.

Courts have ruled that there are only four (4) instances when Social Security numbers MUST be used. These are:

1. For tax purposes

2. To receive public assistance

3. To obtain and use a driver's license

4. To register a motor vehicle

In any situation not listed above, simply present this document to any person who seems to need one. Invite him or her to make a copy. Point out the $1,000 penalty that is guaranteed upon judgment that your rights were violated under this act. Point out that an individual may personally be required to pay the $1,000 if he/she is aware of the Privacy Act and refuses to follow it. In Doyle v. Wilson, the court states: "Assuming that the plaintiff's refusal to disclose his Social Security number was a clearly established right, where defendants could not as reasonable persons have been aware of the right and could not have recognized that any effort to compel disclosure of number or to deny plaintiff his refund violated federal law, damages against defendant were barred." (*Doyle v. Wilson*, D.C., 1982, 529F, Supp 1343.)

It is quite clear that the individuals must be able to show that they could not have been aware of the Privacy Act and could not have possibly realized that their actions were in violation of federal law in order to escape the $1,000 penalty.

Courtesy of the Heritage Caucus

22. Visualize Vermont carry

If the government issued permits for free speech, would you get in line for one? If your local sheriff was willing to grant you permission to practice your religion — after you passed certain tests, gave your fingerprints and let yourself be photographed, would you apply? If your state allowed you to hold a political meeting, but only if you obtained the proper license and consented to having your name entered in a government database, would you lay your money down?

The proper answer is, "We don't need no stinking permits!" Right?

Then you don't need no stinking permit to exercise your right to own and carry firearms, either.

If you ask the government for a *permit*, you are admitting you don't have a right.

If you ask the government for a permit, you are also committing a damn, dumb, dangerous deed. You are helping state governments build what the federal government wants and is forbidden to build for itself — a nationwide registry of gun owners. Worse — it's a registry of those people most likely to *use* guns to defend themselves, their families and their communities against villains of all varieties. These are exactly the people the feds will most want to know about if they ever dare to take the final steps into complete dictatorship.

Haven't you wondered why prominent, federal, anti-gun officials spend very little time fighting and bemoaning the movement for states to issue concealed carry permits? Because it benefits them!

Don't — *ever* — get a concealed carry permit. If you have the courage, bear your gun as you wish. It is your right. Think of it as an act of civil disobedience.

In many western states, concealed carry without a permit is merely a misdemeanor, and one most law enforcement agencies won't even enforce. In other states, like New York, it's a felony and they'll treat you like a murderer for doing it.

If you don't want to break the law, then work to change it. Only one state recognizes the rights of gun owners. Little Vermont has no restrictions on the right to carry firearms, openly or concealed. Gun-rights activists know the system as "Vermont carry." A few states, like Montana and Wyoming which already have a strong gun culture, are probably ripe for its introduction. A few others, like Florida, which have seen the benefits of "allowing" concealed carry, might also eventually be candidates for the more just and radical position.

> *No slave shall keep any arms whatever, nor pass,*
> *unless with written orders from his master or employer,*
> *or in his company, with arms from one place to*
> *another. Arms in possession of a slave contrary to this*
> *prohibition shall be forfeited to him who will seize*
> *them.*
>
> —A Bill Concerning Slaves, Virginia Assembly, 1779

23. Don't talk to strangers

The phone rings.

"Hello?"

"Good evening, I'm with the National Political Porkbarrel League, and I'd like to ask you a few questions about your views on current issues."

"Sure," you say. The next thing you know, after a few innocuous-seeming questions about your name, age and occupation, you're blurting out your opinions on drug legalization, gun control, censorship, abortion, the United Nations, and the legitimate extent of federal police power.

Who are these people, anyway? Why are they doing this? Why are *you* doing this? What's going to happen to this information?

You don't know and you have no way of finding out. This could be anybody calling you. For any purpose. Be paranoid; it's good for you. Don't tell anybody anything, even if they give a convincing story about who they are and how they'll use the information.

Even if you happen to be talking to a legitimate pollster (a rare breed these days, when even old-line organizations like Harris and Gallup are more bent on molding opinion than reporting it), why should you let your ideas, your tooth brushing habits, your car buying patterns or anything else be known to every geek in the universe? What do you gain by it, beyond the momentary satisfaction of having some minimum-wage telephone slave pretend to care?

24. Don't talk to people you know, either

Something like it goes double when you're trying to do business with your banker, your school registrar, the bureaucrat at the drivers license department, your insurance agent, etc.

They give you these forms with the most amazing array of questions. Or they sit at a terminal and grill you through screen after screen. They act as if God himself granted them permission to know everything about your life. Most of us sit there, wanting to open that bank account, attend that school, buy that stereo, get that document, win that contract, etc., believing that if we don't answer, they'll send us away empty handed.

They want more information than ever, now that it's so easy to enter it in a database. When we attempt to halt the information hemorrhage, the human between us and the computer protests, "But the system won't *let* me to leave that field blank!"

Well, big deal. Then the system's got a problem. Tell the human to enter a bunch of zeros or exes, or to list your occupation as "Declined to state." But don't invade your own privacy to appease the gods of The System.

Give them only what *you* think they need to know. Less if you can manage it.

Mass democracy, mass morality and the mass media thrive independently of the individual, who joins them at a cost of at least a partial perversion of his instinct and insights. He pays for his social ease with what used to be called his soul, his discriminations, his uniqueness, his psychic energy, his self.
— Al Alvarez, British writer and poet

25. DO write to your congresscritter

Okay, okay! I said at the top of this book you shouldn't do it, but here's one way to do it, have some fun, possibly get some media attention, and remind your alleged representative that you know what villainy it and its cohorts are perpetrating.

Ask the nice, basic, simple, incredibly polite, unanswerable questions. The monkey-wrench questions. Write them in a tone of bland sincerity, the voice of a trusting citizen who looks to wise leaders for all answers. Then send copies of your letters and their replies (if any) to the local newspaper.

Here are some samples:

"Dear Congressman Mussolini: I guess I am not very sophisticated about government. I've read and read, but I just can't find the place in the Constitution where it says police can take somebody's property and sell it without a court finding anybody guilty of a crime. Would you please tell me what section that's in? I'm sure it must be there, or the police would never do that. Thank you sincerely for your help."

"Dear Representative Brownnose: I see that you voted to keep marijuana illegal. I'm sure you have very good reasons. Would you please send me copies of all the scientific studies showing that marijuana is more harmful than cigarettes or alcohol? Thank you in advance."

"Dear Senator Hooker: You know, it's really funny, but I never hear people say, 'It's a free country,' any more. Isn't that strange? Do you have any idea why? Yours truly."

"Dear Representative Yellowtail: Can you please tell me which guns are okay to own and which I'll get in trouble for? I'm confused, but I'm sure you have an easy way of telling. After all, you congresspeople made the laws, and you wouldn't have made laws we citizens couldn't understand or obey. Please also send me a list of exactly what makes some guns okay and some illegal, so I'll be able to tell for myself in the future. Your help is appreciated."

Copy your letters and the replies to the local newspaper or your favorite and most sympathetic political rag. Pass them around at parties. Start a whole collection. Publish it. Get your friends to write monkey-wrench letters of their own, and compile the hysterical non-answers you receive.

Try the same technique on bureaucrats, heads of political parties, the president, the ambassador to the U.N., and leaders of political causes you detest.

26. Visualize no government

Government only exists because people think it does. If enough of us ignore government — don't obey its laws, don't patronize its services, don't vote for its members, don't fill out its forms...and above all, don't pay the taxes that feed it...it will eventually go away.

Government is only a concept. Concepts change.

As John Lennon didn't sing (but should have), "Imagine there's no government. It isn't hard to do..."

The future is the only kind of property that the masters willingly concede to slaves.
— Albert Camus

27. Fly the Gadsden flag

You've seen it — the bright yellow flag with its coiled rattlesnake and the words, "Don't Tread On Me." That's the Gadsden flag, designed during the American revolution and once a candidate for the role now played by the Stars & Stripes.

It says it all, really: Leave me alone and we can share the same world in peace. Mess with me and I'll strike back — a message every government on earth should get from the best of its citizens — and a message lots of ordinary busybodies should get, too.

Fly the Gadsden flag as a symbol of your attitude — and a reminder that you haven't forgotten the message of the revolution, even if today's King Georges have.
You can order one from:

All Nations Flag Company, Inc.
118 W. Fifth Street
Kansas City, Missouri 64105
voice: 1-800-533-3524
fax: (816) 842-3995
e-mail: gwald@allnationsflags.com
Web site: http://www.allnationsflags.com

As the name implies, this company carries about any flag you could want. Among them are 13-star Old Glories and other flags of the Revolutionary Era. All Nations also carries U.N. flags suitable for burning, if you're into that sort of thing. (Experienced pyro-protesters recommend the cotton version; burning nylon stinks.)

Wherever is found what is called a paternal government, there is found state education. It has been discovered that the best way to insure implicit obedience is to commence tyranny in the nursery.
— Benjamin Disraeli

28. Dare to keep DARE out of your local schools

They're everywhere — those dramatic black-with-red cop cars with the dashing "D.A.R.E" acronym on their sides. DARE — Drug Abuse Resistance Education — is a War on Drugs program sold to the public in a warm, fuzzy, let's save the children cover. "Cover" is the operative word here.

In the decade and more that police have been taking the DARE program to the schools, not one shred of evidence has turned up to show that DARE has discouraged one child from experimenting with drugs. In fact, the psychologist who developed DARE's methods has since disavowed them as completely ineffective.

If the real intent of the program was to encourage children to avoid drugs, why are those DARE cars and DARE cops still invading the schools long after the program has been proven not to work?

Because plenty of evidence has turned up to indicate that DARE is successful at one thing the government wants very much: turning American school kids into little brownshirts, informing on their parents and neighbors "for the good of society."

Some questions:

Did you know that DARE was founded by former L.A. police chief Daryl Gates, who once testified before Congress that every recreational drug user should be shot as a traitor to the War on Drugs?

Did you ever wonder why DARE is being taught by law enforcers, who have only one week of DARE education, instead of by pharmacologists, physiologists, psychologists or physicians with real experience of the effects of drugs?

Do you know that DARE officers have added "anti-violence" messages to their program — which is nothing but the latest warm, fuzzy term for "anybody who owns guns — like your parents, maybe? — is a bad person"?

Do you know that DARE officers are trained to gain the trust of children — expressly to get evidence to arrest the children's family members? The children, who are merely told the police want to "help" their drug-using relatives, often end up in foster homes after finding, to their horror, that they've sent their own parents to jail and lost their own homes and possessions to forfeiture.

DARE isn't and never was a drug abuse prevention program. It was from its inception a political indoctrination program, created by people with minds seething with hate and deviousness.

Even if you have no children, or have been wise enough to pull your kids out of public school, DARE is a threat to you if you use recreational drugs, own firearms, enjoy unorthodox sex play, hold unpopular opinions, or break any of your city, county, state, or country's countless arbitrary laws (as we all do). Your kids might not be brainwashed into finkdom, but that won't help much if the neighbor children have been.

Fight to get your local school district to reject DARE. Fight to get your local police to stop participating in the national program. If nothing else works, use the argument-from-practicality that it's a waste of time and money since it hasn't made a dent in the alleged drug problem.

29. Identify the informant in your midst

If you're involved in any underground or anti-government activity, there is always *one* person you should distrust more than any other. For years, members of groups from the Ku Klux Klan to the Weather Underground have had a saying: "You can always tell the FBI agent; he's the one who keeps trying to get you to bomb something."

It's true.

It just makes sense when you think about it. Most people know violence is a last resort, often as dangerous to the doer as to the victim. Only a tiny handful of fanatics and a huge army of cops eager to advance their careers actually *want* people to initiate violence.

It was an FBI informant who helped a bunch of inept boobs (who couldn't even rent a truck properly) figure out how to bomb the World Trade Center. Then the FBI stood by while the boobs killed people so the feds would look better by having a more serious charge on which to arrest them — a barbarity that didn't seem to bother the media at all.

It isn't only violent crimes cops will urge on you, either.

It was a BATF agent who talked naive, broke Randy Weaver into sawing off two shotguns for a few hundred dollars. The agent worked on Randy for *three years* before he conned him into it, all the while pretending to be a friend. The BATF went to all that effort *not* because they wanted to get Randy, but *only* because they wanted to use Randy's "crime" as leverage to force him into doing the same sort of thing to others! Heck, some 80 percent of the BATF's cases, historically, have involved them entrapping otherwise blameless people.

In general, the feds are outstandingly bad at catching genuine evildoers. Look at the Unabomber case; it wasn't the FBI, it was the suspect's brother who caught him — after 15 years of useless federal investigation!

That's why the feds concentrate instead on manufacturing crimes or catching ordinary people on technicalities; and feds from dozens of agencies — from the IRS, DEA, FBI and BATF to the Immigration and Naturalization Service — are all over the place, doing exactly that, these days.

If we're going to join with other people to fight tyranny we have to act on trust, sometimes, even if we can't be assured we're right. But never be surprised if someone screws you, and *always* believe that the person advocating violence or other law-breaking early, loud and with great persistence is a government agent.

> *Taking my gun away because I might shoot someone is like cutting my tongue out just because I might yell, "Fire!" in a crowded theater.*
> — Peter Venetoklis

30. Remember Mother Batherick

On those days when you feel outnumbered...when you know the tyrants are going to win no matter what you do, remember the people in this little story.

It's true, and it took place on April 19, 1775, the day of the battles of Lexington and Concord. The "embattled farmers" of poetic fame had already begun to rout the well-armed, well-trained redcoats of General Gage. Gage attempted to send two ammunition wagons, accompanied by an officer and 13 grenadiers (the biggest and toughest of soldiers), to resupply his troops, but along the road they ran into a handful of ordinary Americans.

As told by David Hackett Fischer in his wonderful book, *Paul Revere's Ride*:

This little convoy was intercepted on the road by a party of elderly New England men...who were exempt from service with the militia by reason of their age. These gray-headed soldiers did not make a formidable appearance, but they were hardened veterans who made up in experience what they lacked in youth, and were brilliantly led by David Lamson, described as a "mulatto" in the records.

With patience and skill these men laid a cunning ambush for the British ammunition wagons, waited until they approached, and demanded their surrender. The British drivers were not impressed by these superannuated warriors, and responded by whipping their teams forward. The old men opened fire. With careful economy of effort, they systematically shot the lead horses in their traces, killed two sergeants, and wounded the officer in command.

The surviving British soldiers took another look at these old men, and fled for their lives. They ran down the road, threw their weapons into a pond, and started running again. They came upon an old woman named Mother Batherick, so impoverished that she was digging a few weeds from a vacant field for something to eat. The panic-stricken British troops surrendered to her and begged her protection. She led them to the house of militia captain Ephraim Frost.

Mother Batherick may have been poor in material things, but she was rich in the spirit. As she delivered her captives to Captain Frost, she told them, "If you ever live to get back, you tell King George that an old woman took six of his grenadiers prisoner." Afterward, English critics of Lord North's ministry used this episode to teach a lesson in political arithmetic: "If one old Yankee woman can take six grenadiers, how many soldiers will it require to conquer America?"

31. Take your kids out of government school

We live with a myth that compulsory, universal education was established to produce a well-educated populace. Propaganda! Bull-oney! Long before government schools were built, the U.S. had a literacy rate of more than 90 percent, and a population well-versed in history, civics, literature, philosophy and mathematics.

Government schools were, from their inception, designed primarily to keep the children of "the masses" docile (and keep them out of the workplace — a huge national issue at the time compulsory school attendance laws were passed).

America's compulsory education system was the brainchild of U.S. educators who had visited Prussia's highly regimented schools. These edu-controllers had admired the Prussian system's obedient, robot-like students and its philosophy that the state was the true parent of every child. If you doubt it, check out these quotes from some of the founders and philosophers of U.S. government education:

Let our pupil be taught that he does not belong to himself, but that he is public property. He must be taught to amass wealth, but it must be only to increase his power of contributing to the wants and demands of the state. [Education] can be done effectually only by the interference and aid of the Legislature.
— Benjamin Rush (1786)

101 Things to Do 'til The Revolution
48

The secret of the superiority of the state over private education lies in the fact that in the former the teacher is responsible to society...[T]he result desired by the state is a wholly different one than that desired by parents, guardians, and pupils.
— Lester Frank Ward (1897)

[The role of the schoolmaster is to] collect little plastic lumps of human dough from private households and shape them on the social kneading board.
— Edward Ross (1900)

Our schools are, in a sense, factories, in which the raw products (children) are to be shaped and fashioned into products to meet the various demands of life. The specifications for manufacturing come from the demands of twentieth-century civilization, and it is the business of the school to build its pupils according to the specifications laid down.
— Ellwood Cubberley (1920)

Then read *Dumbing Us Down: The Hidden Curriculum in Compulsory Schooling*, by John Taylor Gatto, New Society Publishers, 1992, and *Separating School and State*, by Sheldon Richman, Future of Freedom Foundation, 1994.

You will discover for yourself that today's shocking rates of illiteracy, lack of historic knowledge, and sheeplike belief that people exist to serve the state aren't the result of a system that has *failed*. They are the result of a system that has *succeeded* beyond its founders' wildest hopes.

The system cannot be fixed. It already *works*.

What can you do about it?
Some people imagine school vouchers and charter schools (in which any qualified group can start a school, funded by

the government) promise a way out, but as long as goverment holds the purse strings and has the slightest control over what's taught and how it's taught, the basic problem remains.

Your basic problem, of course, is how to see that your own kids get a diet of healthy information, rather than intellectual junk food — right now. If you're working full-time outside the home, that's a problem. If you're paying an average of several thousand dollars a year in taxes to fund the public schools (some obvious, some hidden in the cost of the items or services you purchase), as most of us are, that's a problem.

Home schooling takes time; private schooling takes money. But help is available.

As more people homeschool, they're developing cooperative groups, great teaching materials and organized classes for their children. There are even on-line schools, operating entirely on the Internet. If you're creative and motivated, you may still be able to homeschool while working outside your home.

Private schools offer scholarships, and many church-based or politically driven schools deliberately keep a very low tuition and offer flexible payment plans.

If you're interested in one of these options, but don't know where to begin, here are some sources of help:

How Do I Homeschool?
SPICE
P.O. Box 282
Wilton, California 95693
e-mail: rab@woozle.emp.unify.com (Ruthann Biel)
    This helpful book is published by a homeschoolers' support group.

National Homeschool Association
P.O. Box 157290
Cincinnati, Ohio 45215-7290
voice: (513) 772-9580
   A national group that may also be able to put you in touch with state or local homeschool groups.

Eagle Academy
Mrs. Jean DeFino, Director of Admissions
49 Violet Ave.
Poughkeepsie, New York 12601-1520
e-mail: eagle@mhv.net
Web site: http://www. eagle.mhv.net
   Eagle Academy is an on-line "school," created for home-schoolers, but open to anyone interested in seeing that their children get a good education.

Growing Without Schooling
2269 Massachusetts Avenue
Cambridge, Massachusetts 92140-1226
voice: (617) 864-3100
e-mail: HoltGWS@erols.com
Web page: http://www.holtgws.com

Separation of School and State Alliance
Marshall Fritz
4578 N. First #310
Fresno, California 93726
voice: (209) 292-1776
fax: (209) 292-7582
Web page: http://www.sepschool.org/
   A political/educational alliance dedicated to getting government out of the education business.

Information about more organizations and publications can be found on the Internet. Try Jon's Home School Resource Page at http://www.midnightbeach.com/, or type the words "home schooling" into any good Internet search engine.

32. Keep your sense of humor

Hey, just because the future of freedom looks grim, that's no reason *you* should. A sense of humor is an essential survival tool in hard times. To keep yourself smiling through it all try:

The Archie McPhee Catalog — There is nothing weirder. Archie McPhee describes itself as "The definitive source for rubber chickens, cheap imported trinkets, weird overstocks and other disgusting, hilarious, fascinating novelties." I might add: voodoo dolls, bubble gum that tastes like pickles, and purple octopi that smell like grape Kool-Aid, glow in the dark and squeak.

Our county Libertarian Party chair always keeps a supply of rubber dog doo on hand, for instance, for those days when opposition tactics get really smelly.

You can get a catalog from:

Archie McPhee and Company
P.O. Box 30852
Seattle, Washington 98103
voice: (425) 745-0711
fax: (425) 745-1743

You can visit their retail store, known as Seattle's Epicenter of Weirdness:

3510 Stone Way North
Seattle, Washington 98103
(206) 545-8344

Or visit them electronically:
Web site: http://www.mcphee.com
E-mail: mcphee@mcphee.com

Weird humor sites on the World Wide Web. These include:
The Mad Martian Museum of Modern Madness (where you'll find the Interactive Toilet of Terror and — I'm not kidding — a genuine, classic hearse for sale):

http://www.madmartian.com

The Temple of Mike. Hard to describe. It's just some guy's thing:

http://www.ucalgary.ca/~mbwarren/temple/index/html

Wutka's Weird Works. Ditto:

http://www.webcom.com/~wutka/welcome.html

The SacredBull Archive of Political Satire and Spoofery. This site, which contains the more light-hearted works of some seriously freedom-loving people (including yours truly) is a companion to the SacredBull e-mail list, maintained by Todd Gillespie. You could think of it as where our satires go to die.

http://users.FoxValley.net/~tgillesp/

The Darwin Awards. There are a number of Darwin Award sites, all highly unofficial, and all featuring tales of people who met Death by Stupidity. This is one of the most complete and funniest Darwin archives.

http://www.dallas.quik.com/grebo/darwin

As I've mentioned elsewhere, Web sites appear and disappear all the time. If you can't find one or more of the above, just type "weird humor" at the prompt in any one of the popular Internet search engines. Something will fly out at you, like an electronic cream pie in the face.

Read anything by P.J. O'Rourke — Anything. *Rolling Stone* columnist, book writer, rock 'n roll Republican, P.J. is one of ours. And funny? Mega-funny!

Pretend you just arrived from another planet and could leave any time you wished — Then think...really think objectively about people like Bob Dole, Bill Clinton, Newt Gingrich, Hillary, Tipper, Charles Schumer, Dianne Feinstein, Pat Buchanan, Jim and Tammy Faye ex-Bakker, Jesse Jackson, Sam Donaldson, Sarah Brady, Ralph Nader, Ralph Reed and — last and definitely least — Louis Farrakhan. They're really the biggest howl on the planet — as long as you don't have to live with the consequences of their actions.

Develop a sense of humor that leaves 'em wondering — Is he for real???

> *When buying and selling are controlled by legislation,*
> *the first things to be bought and sold are legislators.*
> — P.J. O'Rourke

33. Assume all telephones are tapped

When I was in high school, I hung out with a bunch of college radicals who lived together in what they grandly called a commune. It wasn't. It was more like a freelance dorm, but in a state of glorious paranoia, they believed their subversive views had earned them a phone tap. Their standard greeting after picking up the receiver was, "Fuck you, FBI...Hello?"

Well, the FBI probably didn't care, but somebody else did. One commune member was the son of a controversial local politician. A bureaucrat from another faction got their phone tapped in a fishing expedition to embarrass the kid's father.

The guy and his friends were — no surprise — dealing dope, and they all got busted.

Your phone may not be tapped. In fact, the statistics indicate it probably isn't. Phone taps are used only a few thousand times a year in the entire country.

But that is changing.

In 1995 the FBI pushed its Digital Telephony Bill through Congress. It forces every telephone company in the U.S. to build into its system all software and hardware needed to tap every phone in the country easily.

Here is what author Simson Garfinkel, in his book *PGP: Pretty Good Privacy*, had to say about the bill the Clinton administration and its FBI lobbyists worked so hard to pass:

Close inspection of the...bill revealed that it essentially turned control of the nation's communications network over to the Justice Department. At a cost of more than $500 million, it's a move that virtually nationalizes all telephone technology — something unprecedented in U.S. history, except during time of war.

The FBI has also been pushing for Congressional permission to conduct so-called roving wiretaps (so if a friend under surveillance visits your house, they can tap your phone even if you aren't suspected of anything), and wants the capability to snoop on one out of every 100 phone lines in major cities.

Why they imagine there are bad guys in one out of every 100 homes is a provocative question all by itself. Geez, are these guys really *that* paranoid? Or are us dangerous folks really that numerous?

In any case, if you value your freedom, don't say anything on the telephone you wouldn't say to a cop's face. That goes quintuple for your cellphone!

As I write this, there are still some protections on "wired" telephones, but anything you blurt on a cellphone is fair game. Cellphone signals are easy to pick up, and if a cop just "happens" to hear you discuss sharing a joint with your significant other, or opining that you think the president should be "taken out and shot," it's evidence. No search warrant. No nothing. Just free evidence.

So shut up, or if you must say something controversial or illegal, do it on a pay phone. Try to make it a pay phone far from your house, and a different pay phone each time. Keep an eye on the news, because if the feds get their roving wiretaps, pay phones are out, too.

The good news about telephone taps

The good news is that PGP (Pretty Good Privacy), the encryption software that can make your computer communications private, is now available for encrypting telephone conversations. The bad news is that the voice-encryption version is still clunky and not easy to use. That will change in the future. So keep an eye on that news, too. With any luck, the free-enterprise product, PGP, will keep ahead of any counter technique the thundering but thudding bureaucrats of the FBI can get their hands on.

PGP is free and available for downloading from the Internet and computer BBSes. (See *Use PGP intelligently*, No. 41.)

34. Don't debate

Don't argue philosophy or issues with people who disagree with you on fundamentals. Waste of time. You will persuade no one, but rile everyone, including yourself. Don't you have something better to do with your life?

Don't even argue with people who are close to you on issues unless you have good training or instincts for persuasion. Too much risk of alienating a potential ally. Give them some literature, resources and food for thought, then let them "convert" themselves.

The authority of government... can have no pure right over my person and my property but what I concede to it.
— Henry David Thoreau

35. Cover your assets

This book is not written for rich people. Rich people have a thousand ways to hide ownership of their property or stash their assets. They go to Austria and open anonymous accounts, or to Switzerland, where they're known to their bankers discreetly by number. They manage their investments from obscure, but trendy, Caribbean islands. They keep real estate in trusts so deep and many-layered it takes six lawyers to figure out who owns what.

Poor people and middle-class people, whose assets — more scarce — are probably even more precious to them, often get the shaft. Even when they think they're getting good advice from so-called financial privacy advisors, they have few means of verifying how honest or effective that advice is — until it's too late.

However, even us poor folks can, if we look very hard for the right sources, open small international bank accounts, establish inexpensive trusts to hold ownership of our property, and use Visa and MasterCards of a type whose records are not easily accessible to snoops.

(If you care about the legalities, it's perfectly okay as of this writing to keep up to $10,000 total in overseas investments without reporting them to the IRS.)

Here are some sources to which you can turn for information. Please note, I don't expressly recommend any of these. Every financial advisor, in particular, should be viewed with skepticism, and all advice should be subjected to scrutiny. But these are places to start, if you want to try some do-it-yourself asset protection.

The Financial Privacy Report
P.O. Box 1277
Burnsville, Minnesota 55337
voice: (612) 895-8757
fax: (612) 895-5526

This monthly, eight-page newsletter has its plusses and minuses. It's expensive (currently $144 per year, though you can get it for less on special offers). Its publishers or their affiliates will bombard you with sleazy, "Act-now-before-the-world-ends!" offers. Sometimes its writers pad it with background information easily available through political magazines or the Internet. However, it contains enough gems — or leads to gems — that I think it's worth it. It discusses topics such as: offshore bank accounts, anonymous Internet accounts, offshore credit cards, trusts, phone and computer privacy, and protecting your property against forfeiture, and protecting your business against attack by federal eco-police. It gives addresses and other contact information of helpful organizations and businesses, and it always strives to recommend courses of action that are both legal and discreet. If you get just one piece of great information from it, it could save you many times its price.

alt.privacy
   This Internet news group is a good forum for asking questions and getting leads to privacy and asset protection sources.

Canadian banks
Bank of Montreal, Head Office
PO Box 6002, Place D'Armes Postal Station
Montreal, Quebec H2Y 3S8
Canada
voice: (514) 877-7373
fax: (514) 877-9691
Web site: http://www.bmo.com

National Bank of Canada Headquarters
4th Floor, 600 Rue de La Gauchetiere West
Montreal, Quebec H3B 4L2
Canada
voice: (514) 394-6080
fax: (514) 394-8434
Web site: http://www.vse.ca/companies/N/32987s.html

   The Canadian banking system is far from perfect. It doesn't remotely have the privacy of Swiss, Austrian or some Caribbean banks. But it has one big advantage: accessibility to ordinary Americans. To wit:

- You can open an account with very little money either by mail from the U.S., or in person in Canada.
- Most of the account types are familiar enough that you won't require a whole new realm of financial knowledge, as you might with some overseas banks.
- You aren't required to give your Social Security number.
- You can access your money with relative ease.

- You can send deposits to your Canadian account in U.S. dollars without going through any currency swapping hassles.

- In many northern states, you can deposit Canadian funds in your U.S. bank account and the teller will convert the funds with absolutely no fuss and no extra charges.

- In areas near popular U.S./Canadian border crossings you can even write checks on your Canadian account in U.S. stores.

- And even without the privacy guarantees of some other banking systems, it's a big hassle for any U.S. police agency to get information about, or confiscate, your Canadian account.

Swiss banks

Face it, most Swiss banks are beyond your league or mine. For foreign investors, they require minimum balances bigger than most people's annual salaries. But that's not universally true. If you're interested, here are some places to start digging.

400 Swiss Banks!
Web site: http://www.swconsult.ch/chbanks/index.htm

This Internet site lists Swiss banks by canton, by alphabetical order, by whether or not they have Internet sites, and by several other criteria. Unfortunately, it doesn't list them by size of minimum deposit. Some only want to deal with large overseas investors. Last I checked, you could open a Bank Leu account with as little as $1,000. But this changes. Your best course, if you're not wealthy, might be to e-mail several banks on the Internet list and ask about their minimums. This site also contains a link to general information about Switzerland, if you're thinking of visiting or relocating.

400 Swiss Banks! is operated by:
SW Consulting SA
1, chemin du Jura
CH-1292 Chambesy
Switzerland
voice: (+41.22) 758.10.31
fax: (+41.22) 758.33.03
e-mail: info@swconsult.ch

Swiss Investment Market Place
Web site: http://www.jml.ch/jml/jml.html

This site, operated by JML Swiss Investment Counsellors of Zurich, discusses Swiss gold investments, Swiss protected retirement accounts, Swiss banking, international asset protection trusts and other things most of us probably aren't in the right league for. JML will also sell you its advice and assistance on Swiss investing — if you're in a much bigger league than the very, very little one I play in. However, there's lots of info here and JML will send you free information on their seminars, plus a free trial subscription to their newsletter.

More confidential Visa and MasterCards

Those purchase-by-purchase records your credit card company sends you every month are also available to police agencies and the IRS. With them, they can estimate your income, find out where you've been traveling, learn your tastes in goodies, and make guesses about whether you've been up to anything illegal. If you have to run from the law using a credit card, the cops can follow right in your tracks and catch you.

Besides all that, they can just snoop into your perfectly ordinary life — which they have no damn business doing.

You can make that impossible, or at least very much more difficult, by using debit cards from certain offshore banks — thus putting your purchase records under the jurisdiction of a foreign government. Some of these will only cooperate with U.S. officials in the most heinous of criminal cases. Some absolutely refuse to cooperate with U.S. officials on any tax matters.

Visa and MasterCard debit cards, as you may know, look just like regular credit cards, but they draw against funds you have on deposit. There's no actual credit involved. If you have $1,200 in the bank, you can make $1,200 worth of purchases. Deposit more, make more purchases. It's like writing a check, except that businesses accept them like credit cards. You can easily make U.S. purchases, even though your account may be based in English pounds, or some other currency, and there are no horrendous interest charges, since you're using your own money.

One overseas bank issuing these cards is:

TSB Bank Channel Islands
P.O. Box 597
St. Helier, Jersey,
Channel Islands
voice: 011-441-534-27306
fax: 011-441-534-23058

• Request information about their TSB Bankcard and Off-shore Premium Account. They do have a minimum deposit equal to about $3,000 U.S. Your account will be in British pounds — which could be a drawback or a benefit, depending on currency fluctuations. This bank has been in business since the early 1800s, and while nobody can guarantee the safety of any bank, if you charge a few thousand dollars a year on your credit card anyway, it's worth the small financial risk to have the extra privacy.

The bank can explain to you how to send your initial deposit.

It will be of little avail to people that the laws are made by men of their own choice, if the laws be so voluminous that they cannot be understood; or if they be repealed or revised before they are promulgated, or undergo such incessant changes that no man knows what it will be tomorrow.... Frequent changes give an unreasonable advantage to the sagacious, enterprising, and the moneyed few, over the industrious and uninformed mass of the people.
— James Madison

36. Expect to lose everything, anyway

You may not have time to hide your assets effectively before tyranny rampages in your direction in the shape of the IRS, DEA, BATF or some other scrambled alphabet police agency. Simple economics may get you first.

Your efforts to hide what you own may be blown away. Today's fail-safe methods become tomorrow's traps as laws and regulations change. A single compromised official blows the security of a whole "confidential" banking system. The method you chose turns out to be based on bad information — and the "advisor" who sold you on the idea is long gone.

Realize that, despite your best efforts, you could lose all your possessions — house, car, bank accounts, retirement plan — all of it. Overnight.

So prepare yourself to lose. This suggestion has two parts. One involves preparing yourself mentally for the worst. The other involves some steps to help keep the worst from happening.

Imagining the worst

First, spend some time imagining scenarios in which you might find yourself broke, homeless, desperately in debt or whatever. Prepare yourself mentally and emotionally. Think about what your options might be.

- Would you have anyone to turn to for help?
- Are you capable of living on the street, if need be?
- Could you survive the climate where you live? And if not, could you get quickly to another part of the country?
- Have you got an alternate place to sleep — even a travel trailer, van, cave or tent?
- How would you reach help if your car was taken?
- How would you communicate if your computer had been seized? (And would you have backup files in a secure place?)
- How would you feed & clothe your children, or take care of the medical problems of a family member?

Whatever your situation, think it out and be as ready as you can for it, physically, emotionally and intellectually.

Preparing for the worst

Second, to minimize some of the impact, make sure you have at least minimal plans in reserve and minimal stashes of resources in safe places. For instance:

- If you rely on your computer, place duplicate diskettes with a trusted friend or relative, but one not closely involved with your political activities. A person too close to you might be busted at the same time you are.
- Bury a small survival kit, including clothes, weapons, food, medical supplies, and negotiable money somewhere away from your property. (See *Bury gold, guns and goodies,* No. 97.) It will come in handy if the government

seizes everything else you own, or if you must make a run for it, for whatever reason.

- If you anticipate being on the run or stranded in poverty with pets, children, sick family members or elderly relatives, do your best to lay aside items they'll need (See *Prepare your children, pets, and aging relatives*, No. 85). Put those items in a secure place, preferably off your property.

- Arrange emergency shelter in advance with a friend or relative — or scope out a useable camping spot on remote public land.

- Deposit a few hundred dollars or a few thousand dollars in a checking account in a Canadian bank. Maybe open two or three such accounts. (See #35 above.) That extra stash — not easy for the government to grab — may help you survive in the first weeks or months after a property seizure or other government-caused disaster.

- Develop some survival skills appropriate to the scenarios you envision for yourself.

- Learn to do with less — now.

Preparing for disaster is an enormous task. If you're young or poor (or both), it's especially daunting. The sheer number of things you need to think about is awesome, and the money needed to prepare thoroughly is beyond most of us.

But remember — doing *some* things is better than doing nothing. Even if all you can do is prepare *mentally*, you're still better off than if you never prepared at all.

Above all, do not allow the loss of mere material possessions to submerge you in depression. The name of the game is survival, and that means mental and emotional survival, as well as physical. You can always recover from the loss of *things*. You may never recover if you let tyrants destroy your *self*.

If you can survive as a whole person when the government believes it has taken *everything* from you, you win. With nothing left to lose, you are in a position to fight harder than ever for freedom.

Stay alive! Survive to become a tyrant's worst enemy.

When you ain't got nothin', you got nothin' to lose. You're invisible now...
— Bob Dylan

37. Respect individuals, not groups

There is not a group on this planet worthy of your respect. Only individuals. Respect or disrespect them case-by-case, based on what they do, not what categories they belong to.

It's possible that your greatest ally could be a DEA or BATF agent becoming disillusioned with the agency's practices. It's possible your worst enemy could be a friend about to rat on you to save his or her own butt. It's possible that the smartest person you'll ever meet will be a member of a racial group you always believed was stupid. It's possible that the most venal person you'll ever meet belongs to a group otherwise known for its honor.

There's another aspect of this group thing, too.

Groups develop what my friend Kevin calls a "synergistic personality." Kevin points out that the Democrats he knows as individuals aren't at all the Democrats he knows when they're acting as a group. People who would never steal from him or force him to obey their will as individuals band together and insist he obey them "for the common good."

Somehow groups give individuals "permission" to be more ruthless, more dictatorial, more self-righteous than the same person would be when facing you one-to-one. But the individual is still responsible. The individual is still the doer of the group's deeds.

Besides all this, remember the wise words of Groucho Marx: "I wouldn't belong to any group that would have me as a member."

The only freedom which deserves the name is that of pursuing our own good in our own way.
— John Stuart Mill

The next four sections are specifically for people who have recently entered — or want to enter — the telecommunications loop. If you aren't a computer user, you might want to skip these items — or better yet, consider getting wired in.

38. Fun and freedom on the Internet

The Internet is the most subversive thing going today — and living proof that free-market anarchy works. It enables you to exchange information with anyone, anywhere in the world, for almost any purpose. It lets you spend your time in virtual communities made up of the neighbors you personally choose. The electronic realm is very much the kind of "world" most of us would choose to live in if we could — with entirely voluntary relationships and little or no government.

The Internet (like its independent cousins such as Fidonet) has no president, CEO, director, king or pope. It has no capitol, no headquarters, no laws, no regulations, no corporate policies — only some mutually agreed-upon standards and procedures for providers, site developers and engineers. It collects no taxes. It holds no threats over our heads. It imprisons no violators. It just works.

The Internet is, furthermore, a haven and breeding ground for libertarian and anarchist thinking. It is our realm — the realm in which, despite attempts at federal regulation, we are still free.

There are three major things you can do on the Internet:

- Browse the Web — that is, link with other computers to look at photos, read information, order books, join organizations, and in some cases, grab text, photos and even sounds and video clips and take them from the host computer into yours, for keeps.
- Send and receive electronic mail to other individuals.
- Participate in Usenet groups, also called newsgroups or forums. These are just a kind of mass e-mail, where you send and receive messages that can be read by all the participants in the group. (As opposed to regular e-mail, which is private communication between you and one or more individuals you personally choose.) You can also subscribe to Internet lists, which work slightly differently, but accomplish pretty much the same thing as newsgroups.

If you aren't already on the Internet, all of the above might not make much sense. Unfortunately, there isn't room in this book for even a basic primer on computers and telecommunications. The best thing I can say is — Just Do It.

Starting to browse

All you need is a fairly modern computer, a modem, an Internet service provider, and a software package that will let you dial up and browse. Any computer store or friendly computer user can tell you what you need and even set you up to begin.

Once the hardware and software are installed, it won't take you long to be using the net like a pro. The software dials the phone number of your service provider, and there you are. Using the Internet is simpler and faster than using your library's catalog — and there's a lot more to find!

Once on line, there are two ways to get around. The easiest is to use a search engine — which is something like an electronic catalog or index. Don't worry about buying one; your software will come with several. They're easier to use than print indexes or catalogs, because they do the searching for you. Just type in key words for what you're looking for — "tax havens," "anarchism," "gun rights," "drug legalization," "homeschooling," "revolution," etc. The software will toss up information on a number of possible sites for you to go to. Click on the one (or ones) that sounds best — and go.

The other way to get around — a little less easy, but more reliable — is to type in the URL of the Internet location you're looking for. Yes, I know that sounds horrible. URL sounds like some obscure, difficult thing only a computer nerd could possibly deal with. But believe me, it isn't. A URL (Universal Resource Locator) is nothing more than an electronic address. Type it in, just as you'd type an address on an envelope, hit return — and you're off. The next thing you know, your computer is connected to one in Albuquerque, New Mexico or Copenhagen, Denmark.

(There's no long distance charge for hopping all over the world, either. Normally, the only charge is your provider's monthly fee. Phone fees only come into it if your provider is located outside your free calling area, and then you pay only to connect to the provider, not to all those folks in Sweden and Australia.)

Some URLs to get you started

URLs are addresses. So it makes sense that they take you to sites, or places (also called "pages"). On those pages, you'll find some of the text highlighted in colors. When you click your cursor on highlighted areas, you go to other places, which may be on the same computer — or halfway around the globe. A political organization, for instance, might offer you links to the Web pages of a dozen or more other organizations with similar missions.

The vast array of "links" between sites will help you quick-y find and develop your own collection of favorite places. (Believe me, no matter how confusing it sounds now, this will be the easiest thing you've ever done, once you've got your hands on the keys.)

In the meantime, here are a few of mine to get you started. You've already seen others scattered throughout this book everywhere more conventional "snail" mail addresses appear.

The Vindex — Collected columns of syndicated libertarian writer Vin Suprynowicz:

http://www.nguworld.com/vindex/index.html

Amazon.com Books! — The biggest bookstore in the world, with more than a million titles:

http://www.amazon.com

The Constitution Society — The finest archive of U.S. historical and legal documents on the Internet. Also features a large array of links to other political sites concerned with freedom and the Constitution:

http://www.constitution.org

Claire Wolfe archives — My 'net friends Mary Lou Seymour and Doc Memory were kind enough to put up archives of my writings. I also have a web site of my own that includes the writings of many contemporary freedom lovers.

Mary Lou's Liberty Activist site:

http://www.geocities.com/CapitolHill/Lobby/1797/essay.html

Doc Memory's Knox Free Voice:

http://www.public.usit.net/marchese

Wolfe's Lodge:

http://www/geocities.com/SoHo/Lofts/2110

Oceania: The Atlantis Project — A look at a man-made libertarian paradise that might actually be built someday. There's some fun stuff on this site, like the "Oceania Spy Network," which you can join, and a trivia quiz:

http://www.oceania.org

Electronic Frontier Foundation — Founded by Grateful Dead lyricist and famed computer nerd John Perry Barlow, EFF is fighting in a loud, clear, uncompromising and utterly libertarian voice against government attempts to control the Internet. Barlow says — and rightly so — that governments, with their overarching desire for central control and their roots in the past, can't even understand the net, let alone govern it. For great information on net freedom, covering the entire world:

http://www/eff.org

Cypherpunks — The Cypherpunks are a group based at the University of California, Berkeley and dedicated to encryption and other aspects of cyberspace freedom:

http://www.csua.berkeley.edu/cypherpunks/

Subrosa — Subrosa is a darned good freedom-and-gun-rights site. But the very best thing about Subrosa is its dozens and dozens of other links to the pages of pro-freedom groups:

http://rrnet.com/~subrosa/freedom.html

The Satires of Patty Neill — The witty works of political satirist Patty Neill can be found at a number of web sites. Two "Patty" sites that are highly entertaining and provocative in their own right are:

http://redmon.deltos.com/ (Fratricide) and
http://geocities.com/SoHo/Lofts/2110/Neill.html
    (Wolfe's Lodge)

FBI Home Page — Visit the FBI to learn the latest twist on their paranoid views, learn what new powers they want from Congress, and pick up reports on new investigative technologies. Once you're there, however, you might just find yourself feeling like a Junior G-Person as you explore their "10 Most Wanted" page and their latest hot investigations:

http://www.fbi.gov

Jeff Chan's gun rights archives — This site, maintained by one dedicated individual, is one of the net's most comprehensive sites for articles, statistics and other information pertaining to gun rights:

http://rkba.org

Drugs and Drug Users — A good informational site for anyone interested in contemporary political issues around drugs, also for anyone who wants realistic information about the effects of drugs, without anti-drug hype:

http://www.paranoia.com/drugs

Project Gutenberg — Bless these dedicated people; their goal is to put 10,000 books, mostly classics, into electronic form and make them available, free, over the Internet. The only problem with the Gutenberg web site is that so many people access it, and the books available there take so long to download, that it is darned near impossible to get on. Many other sites carry one or more of the project's books, however, and subsidiary Gutenberg sites are developing as universities pick up the Gutenberg library and make it available from their own facilities:

http://www.promo.net/pg/_titles/_A_index.html

International Society for Individual Liberty — ISIL takes the "Tom Paine approach" to liberty, with more than a million copies of their liberty-oriented pamphlets in print. ISIL also holds an annual conference to discuss the issues of freedom:

http://creative.net/~star/

Liberty Round Table — This is a site for people making active, individual (and sometimes quite entertaining) plans for liberty. There's an associated discussion group, whose address you'll find on the site:

http://home.utah-inter.net/don-tiggre/lrthp.htm

Youkali People — This one's just for fun. I don't know the history, but it looks as if a bunch of kids (and some older people, too) dreamed up an imaginary island and are peopling it with themselves and their friends. A delightful fantasy world:

http://www.via.net:80/~verdi/ppl.html

Hodge Podge Transformer — If you're interested in Discordianism (a religion masquerading as a joke or a joke masquerading as a religion), this is the place for you:

http://www.math.grin.edu/~hamilton/fnord/hodge.html

Advocates for Self-Government — This group of liber-tarians is dedicated to helping people communicate their pro-liberty views more effectively. They publish The World's Smallest Political Quiz (with four corners, not merely right and left sides) and run Operation Politically Homeless to help proto-libertarians find their philosophical homeland. You can download an electronic version of the quiz from their site and set it up on your own computer:

http://www.self-gov.org

Important note: Web sites come and go. Anyone can put up a page and thousands of individuals and organizations do. (Your own Web provider will probably make it possible for you to put up your own. Publish your job resume on it, or post an essay about Truth, Justice and the American Way — whatever you want.) This also means people frequently lose interest in their pages, move them to another site, change the subject matter, or do a lot of other things to make sites somewhat less durable than Mt. Rushmore. If you're looking for a particular type of information and the URL doesn't work any more, go back to the search engines and type in the topic.

Secrecy is the keystone of all tyranny. Not force, but secrecy...censorship. When any government, or any church, for that matter, undertakes to say to its subjects, "This you may not read, this you must not see, this you are forbidden to know," the end result is tyranny and oppression, no matter how holy the motives. Mighty little force is needed to control a man whose mind has been hoodwinked; contrariwise, no amount of force can control a free man, a man whose mind is free. No, not the rack, not fission bombs, not

anything. You cannot conquer a free man; the most you can do is kill him.
— Robert A. Heinlein, *Revolt in 2100*

39. Don't say anything you don't want the world to remember

Did you know that all traffic on all Usenet (Internet) newsgroups is archived? Every word you ever "speak" on alt.politics.guns, alt.revolution, alt.sex.homosexual, alt.anger or any other discussion group is stored.

So don't say anything you might regret in four or five years.

On the other hand...

40. Throw key words into your e-mail

There are some provocative words you should "speak" electronically just for the hell of it. Here's why.

Federal agencies regularly monitor electronic transmissions that leave the borders of the U.S. There are restrictions on their ability to monitor domestic telecommunications; but don't imagine they don't do it.

It's impossible for human beings to scan for all possibly "subversive" or "criminal" messages flying back and forth on computer networks. So computers do the scanning, looking for key words.

Such words might be: assassinate, assassination, bombing, bomb, explosive, amphetamine, cocaine, joint, sinsemilla, hemp, Columbia, murder, kill, meth lab, crank, hit, terrorism, crack, connection or C4, Swiss account, along with names of various other drugs, drug-making chemicals, explosive chemicals, guns and gun parts, "suspicious" financial terms, sexual terms, etc. The actual words being scanned for will change, depending on which "crimes" the feds are hot for at the moment.

If you deliberately attach these words to otherwise innocuous e-mail messages, you help overload the fedsnoop system, twit the snoopers, and make a free speech protest without endangering yourself. Add them to your signature line or send every message with an extra line like, "Net Nazi boob bait term for the day: revolution."

You may even be able to find some free software to add trigger words to your messages automatically. I'm not aware of any for DOS, Windows or Mac — yet — but Unix programmers have written some, and versions that work with your software may not be far behind.

> *Random action produces random political results. Why waste even a rock?*
> — Abbie Hoffman in *Steal This Book*

41. Use PGP intelligently

PGP — Pretty Good Privacy — is encryption software you can use to keep your e-mail messages and other computerized documents from snoopy noses. It's free for non-commercial uses. Anybody can download it from the Internet or a computer bulletin board and install it on their system. So far, no one has even come close to breaking it.

You can get it from the Web at

http://web.mit.edu/network/pgp-form.html

The "mit.edu" part of the URL tells you you're logging onto a computer at Massachusetts Institute of Technology. Since MIT is the official home of PGP, you can count on their site being around longer than most.

To download PGP from there, you'll have to tell their computer you are calling from within the U.S. and that you are a citizen or legal alien. All this is necessary because of yet another asinine federal law (see below). There's nothing to prevent you lying. But if you're uncomfortable with that (or worried they'll keep a record of your call), you can also get PGP from any friend who uses it, and from a lot of other politically oriented Internet sites and private computer bulletin boards.

To learn to use it to best advantage, read *PGP: Pretty Good Privacy*, by Simson Garfinkel, O'Reilly & Associates, Inc., Sebastopol, California, 1995. (Available at any good book store.)

PGP can do more than encrypt your messages. People who receive your messages can also use it: 1) to verify that the message is indeed from you; and, 2) to make sure the message hasn't been corrupted — accidentally or deliberately — during transmission.

Keep a few things in mind:

- PGP requires that both you and the people who receive your messages possess electronic "keys." The program will generate them but you will need to provide them to your correspondents.
- Use of PGP could attract government attention. Cops may not be able to read your messages, but the mere fact that the messages are encrypted could trigger their suspicions. (Not likely; too many people are using it now; but it's possible.)
- Use it consistently, if you're going to use it at all; encrypting some messages and not others could be a clue that you have something specific to hide, rather than just a general desire for privacy.

- Finally, the U.S. government considers PGP a *munition.*
(Well, why not? Any government weird enough to bring a
lawsuit against $405,089.23 or someone's house is pre-
cisely irrational enough to imagine a piece of software is a
bazooka.) Thus, you are committing a federal crime if you
"export" it. So if you send the PGP code to a European
friend, post it on an Internet site without limiting access
to U.S. callers, or cross international borders carrying
your computer with PGP installed, you could be in
trouble. Sending encrypted messages across international
borders is still perfectly legal, since you aren't "export-
ing" the encryption software itself.

The more ridiculous a belief system, the higher the
probability of its success.
— Wayne R. Bartz

42. Challenge all assumptions

There's a lot of bullshit going around: Propaganda, Dis-
information, Misunderstood information, Haywire opinion,
Bent facts, Misinterpreted facts, Urban legends, Paranoid
fantasy, and Eyewitness accounts by people who didn't really
see what they think they saw.

When evaluating information, remember: The sun doesn't
rise in the east unless you personally see it do so.

And even then — it doesn't really rise in the east, does it?
It only appears to because of the rotation of the earth.

Nothing is what it seems. Nothing should be accepted at
face value.

If all mankind minus one were of one opinion, and
only one person were of the contrary opinion, mankind
would be no more justified in silencing that one person

than he, if he had the power, would be justified in silencing mankind.
  —John Stuart Mill

43. Move to a small town

In times of trouble, where's the best place to be?

Sure as hell not in any major urban area. Disaster strikes urban areas every day in the form of gridlock, bureaucracy, air pollution, crime and general inhumanity; it's just that the inhabitants are so used to it they've forgotten the way they live isn't "normal."

By the same token, a bunker mentality won't do you much good, either. Retreating to the hills didn't help Vicki and Randy Weaver. Living on a farm surrounded with barbed wire didn't do the Montana freemen much good.

Rural areas are fine if you cherish the lifestyle, but don't imagine isolation alone will protect you.

If you're planning to relocate, keep your eye on small cities and towns — say, anything from a hundred inhabitants to 5,000. Maybe as large as 50,000 — as long as you are talking independent communities, not mere suburban warts on big city butts.

In communities of this size, you'll find a variety of skills and trading opportunities useful in hard times, but you'll also find a sense of community that means you're less likely to get looted or shot at in a crisis. Small cities out of the population mainstream are also likely to be have a larger share of people who share your disgruntled political views.

I'm not saying small towns are perfect. There's always the problem of everyone knowing your business. They can be boring, too. It's just an option.

Read

   The next seven items are all about books and magazines. As I was making my lists of recommended books on the topics of getting around the system, self-sufficiency and fighting, I found myself recommending books from Loompanics Unlimited to the point where I worried you'd think I was shamelessly plugging and toadying to my own publisher.

   But there you have it. Loompanics (and after Loompanics, Paladin Press — also plugged below) is the best source for titles Waldenbooks and B. Dalton would quail at carrying.

44. Read: fiction

   This list doesn't pretend to be comprehensive; these books are just some of my favorites and good starters for a liberty library. Commonly available titles are listed by title and author only. Where a book is harder to find, I've given as much information as possible to help you locate it.

The Moon is a Harsh Mistress, by Robert Heinlein. This has been described as how the American Revolution might have been fought on the moon.

Atlas Shrugged, by Ayn Rand. The great novel of freedom. A bit dated, a bit talky, a bit...well, Ayn Randish. But there's still nothing like it to stir both mind and spirit. Rand's other works, fiction and non-fiction, deserve a read, too, whether or not you entirely agree with her philosophy or entirely like her attitude.

The Monkey Wrench Gang, by Edward Abbey. This is the novel that inspired the Earth First! movement of outlaw eco-protection. You may like it or loathe it, but there's a lot to be learned from it.

The Probability Broach, by L. Neil Smith. This rousing libertarian science fiction adventure was first published in

1980 and has been almost impossible to find since. However, in October 1996, it was re-issued with new material. This is the story of a weary, middle-aged Denver police detective Win Bear, suddenly catapulted from the crime-ridden, bureaucracy-ridden, unfree United States into the parallel universe of the North American Confederacy, where no federal government exists, freedom prevails, and people of his age are glowing with youth. Neil also wrote several other North American Confederacy novels (notably *The Venus Belt*) and has produced many other freedom-oriented science fiction novels. But in my humble opinion (Sorry, Neil!) none come close to this one.

Illuminatus!, by Robert Shea and Robert Anton Wilson. This wonderful, weird trilogy (*The Eye in the Pyramid*, *The Golden Apple*, and *Leviathan*) is both a liberating mind trip and a surrealistic tale in which every conspiracy theory you ever heard is true — especially the conflicting ones. If you like this, try anything else by Wilson (Fiction and non-fiction — With him, it can be hard to tell which is which.), then go on to explore Discordianism. (Is it a joke disguised as a religion? Or a religion disguised as a joke?) The Loompanics Unlimited catalog is a good source.

Kings Of The High Frontier, by Victor Koman, Pulpless.com. 1996. This magnificent new novel about the death of NASA and the birth of a private space race is written from a hard-core anarcho-libertarian perspective. While too many books have been hyped as "the greatest novel of freedom since *Atlas Shrugged*," this one finally deserves praise. (And unlike Rand, Koman spares us the 65-page speeches. If you feel like giving up on Planet

Earth, *Kings* will give you hope for the future in space. As of this writing, it's available only in electronic form from http://www.pulpless.com. You may pay on-line via credit card or e-cash. Other payment methods are available by arrangement with the Pulpless.Com's webmaster, J. Neil Schulman. And the book is worth whatever you have to go through to get it. (From the author of two other thought-provoking libertarian novels, *The Jehovah Contract* and *Solomon's Knife*.)

45. Read: history

History books are usually as dull as a Bill Clinton speech, so I've recommended only those that are readable as well as full of good information. This list also makes no attempt to be comprehensive, and tends to cover small segments of history rather than attempting a big picture. But again, these books are good starters.

Paul Revere's Ride, by David Hackett Fischer, Oxford University Press, 1994. The most comprehensive account available of the famous ride and the Battles of Lexington and Concord. Besides that, it's an absolutely delightful read.

Albion's Seed, by David Hackett Fischer, Oxford University Press, 1989. A fascinating account of early U.S. cultural history. Hackett shows that English settlement was by four cultural groups with distinctly different origins, habits and philosophies — and that these differences are still reflected today in our own culture. (Ever wonder why the politics of the mid-Atlantic states are so different than the rest of the nation? This book will help you begin to understand why.)

The Whiskey Rebellion: Frontier Epilogue to the American Revolution, by Thomas Slaughter, Oxford University Press, 1988. First thing on the agenda after the American Revolution was — guess what? — a tax revolt. The rebels lost, and that has a lot to do with how we eventually became a nation of the government, by the government and for the government.

Story of a Secret State, by Jan Karski, Houghton Mifflin Company, Boston, 1944. An account of life in the Polish Underground during World War II. Out of print and very hard to find — but worth it.

John Adams and the American Revolution, by Catherine Drinker Bowen, Little, Brown and Company, Boston, 1950. An excellent, very readable account of activities at the heart of the Revolution. Also out of print, but likely to be hiding at your local library.

The South Was Right!, by James Ronald Kennedy and Walter Donald Kennedy, 1994. (Available by mail from Loompanics Unlimited.) This book busts the myths of the Civil War and looks at the war's lasting effects on our country. If you learned in school that millions of southerners went to war so that a handful of rich folks could own slaves, you learned a very silly thing. Find out what the real issues were in this well-documented, but challenging book.

The Battle of Athens, Tennessee, by C. Stephen Byrum, Paidia Productions, Chattanooga, Tennessee, 1987. (Available by mail order from Jews for the Preservation of Firearms Ownership, 2872 S. Wentworth Avenue, Milwaukee, Wisconsin 53207, voice: (414) 769-0760, fax: (414) 483-8435.) This book tells the little known, but well-documented story of how a group of returning World War II GI's re-took their county by force of arms after finding the local government under the control of a corrupt sheriff. After fighting for freedom in Europe, they weren't about to put up with tyranny in their own town. A great argument for the Second Amendment and an interesting story of a successful rebellion against abusive authority.

The Discovery of Freedom, by Rose Wilder Lane. (Available by mail from Laissez Faire Books, San Francisco, address below.) As its title implies, this book is about the history of freedom and the cultural conditions that promote freedom. Gracefully written by the daughter of Laura Ingalls Wilder (who was also, secretly, the primary author of the "Little House" books).

In all ages hypocrites, called priests, have put crowns on the heads of thieves, called kings.
— Robert Ingersoll

46. Read: Founding Fathers & philosophers of freedom

The Declaration of Independence, by Thomas Jefferson.

The U.S. Constitution and Bill of Rights.

Common Sense, by Thomas Paine.

The Federalist Papers. (Commonly available in several editions.) The classic arguments by James Madison, John Jay and Alexander Hamilton in favor of the U.S. Constitution.

The Anti-Federalist Papers, edited by Ralph Ketcham, New American Library, 1986. Ironically, modern people who want to show what the Founding Fathers were all about usually point to the *Federalist Papers*. However, those were written by the "big government" advocates of their day. Another faction — consisting of Thomas Jefferson, Patrick Henry and others we more closely identify with the Revolution, opposed the writing of the Constitution and creation of a strong central government. Here's the book that tells why.

Democracy in America, by Alexis de Tocqueville. This is the brilliant analysis of American culture and government written some 50 years after the Revolution by a politically astute visitor to our country. De Tocqueville predicted many of the things that would happen to our political system, and his insights are worth reading today. (By the way, unlike Bill Clinton and his ilk, de Tocqueville was educated enough to understand that this country's form of government is a constitutional republic, not a democracy. He uses the term democracy, properly, to differentiate a power-to-the-people cultural system from that of one run by nobles.)

The Law, by Frederic Bastiat, The Foundation for Economic Education, Inc., Irvington-on-Hudson, New York. (Available by mail from sources listed on page 192.) The classic essay on limited government, written by a French economist and statesman to counter the socialist ideas of the Paris Commune of 1848.

On Civil Disobedience, by Henry David Thoreau. Philosophical grounding for anyone who says NO to government.

No Treason: The Constitution of No Authority, by Lysander Spooner. (Available by mail from Loompanics Unlimited.)

Why the Constitution doesn't apply to thee and me, by a crotchety, 19th century anarchist philosopher who once ran his own postal system.

For other books and pamphlets on liberty, see Appendix I on page 192.

Laissez Faire Books. These guys have lots more titles on various themes of liberty — economics, politics, fiction, philosophy, humor, and contemporary issues. Contact them at:

Laissez Faire Books
938 Howard Street, Suite 202
San Francisco, California 94103
voice: (415) 541-9780
orders: 1-800-326-0996
fax: (415) 541-9780
Web site: http://www.lfb.org

> *It is error alone which needs support of government.*
> *Truth can stand by itself.*
> — Thomas Jefferson

47. Read: monkey wrenching & getting around the system

One thing this world needs is a great book on monkey wrenching. We could use more information on insidious little ways to damage government property or undermine the credibility of institutions.

Admittedly, some institutions are doing an excellent job of undermining their own credibility these days, but they could use our help.

Alas, this is an area where even the Loompanics Unlimited catalog falls short of perfection. Monkey wrenching, while widely practiced on a "freelance" basis, has not yet found its bible, its code of non-ethics, its ultimate how-to manual.

The best (if imperfect) monkey wrenching book

The best monkey wrenching book is still the original: *Ecodefense*, by Dave Foreman and Bill Haywood (Abbzug Press, Chico, California). This is the basic manual for Earth First! There's a lot to disagree with in the book's philosophy, but a lot to learn from its detailed and exacting sabotage techniques. The biggest drawback is that the book's methods are specific to the timber industry and other corporate "destroyers of nature." *Ecodefense* is a how-to for tree-spiking, survey-marker moving, and sabotage of logging equipment. I'm rather fond of the timber industry, actually, and found this all to be nasty stuff. On the other hand, the techniques that can cripple a logging shovel or skidder can just as easily put a crimp in the action of an IRS agent's car or a fedgoon's HumVee. Worth a look.

Now, will someone please write *FreeCoDefense: A Manual on Restoring America?*

Loompanics does carry one inspirational book on the subject. *Pranks!*, by Re/Search, examines how artists and off-the-wall political figures like Abbie Hoffman, Paul Krassner and Timothy Leary have used pranks to bend "reality," undermine perceptions of "truth," and implant a healthy distrust of institutions.

And more monkey wrenching

Loompanics does carry a good selection of books on revenge. I don't favor revenge, as a personal matter. When you go for payback after a nasty divorce or a squabble with a neighbor, I think you degrade yourself far more than you harm the other person. You waste your own future by focusing it on some loser or jerk's past deeds. You admit that guy's life is more important to you than your own.

BUT, when you're caught in the grip of a vicious beast that won't let you go... a monster that's determined to stop you from having a peaceful, free future anyway... a government that's escaped all reasonable limits... then revenge techniques serve a purpose. The purpose isn't revenge for the past, but sabotage in the present to gain freedom in the future. Now, that's worthwhile.

So while it might be a waste of energy to (for instance) buy a subscription to a gay magazine in the name of your ex-best friend, but put his next-door neighbor's address on it "by mistake," it could be just dandy to do the same thing to an IRS agent or a pompous political figure known for his gay-bashing.

Anyway, here are some books with ideas on the best, most vicious dirty tricks. All are available from Loompanics:

* *Gaslighting: How to Drive Your Enemies Crazy*, by Victor Santoro;
* *Take No Prisoners: Destroying Enemies with Dirty and Malicious Tricks*, by Mack Nasty;
* *Get Even* and *Get Even 2*, both by George Hayduke, the acknowledged master of the field.

Getting around the system

Loompanics has a good selection of books on personally getting around the system, too. These include, as a sampling:

* *Understanding U.S. Identity Documents*, by John Q. Newman;
* *How To Legally Obtain a Second Citizenship and Passport*, by Adam Starchild;
* *Reborn in Canada*, by Trent Sands;
* *Birth Certificate Fraud* (reprint of a government document);
* *Counterfeit I.D. Made Easy*, by Jack Luger;

- *Scram: Relocating Under a New Identity*, by James S. Martin.

Don't automatically trust what you read on these subjects. Laws change. Ways of detecting false documents become more sophisticated and, frankly, some people who write on these topics don't appear to know what they're talking about. It could be helpful to read two or three different books, then check them against information from government agencies, magazines and the real-world experience of people who've done it.

"A well-educated electorate being necessary to the security of a free State, the right of the people to keep and read books shall not be infringed."

Does that mean only well-educated people have a right to own and read books? Then how can this:

"A well-regulated militia being necessary to the security of a free State, the right of the people to keep and bear arms shall not be infringed"

...possibly mean only members of the militia have a right to own weapons?

48. Read: self-reliance

Here's another good starter list — with leads to lots more. This one includes a magazine and a newsletter, as well as books.

Backwoods Home. This bi-monthly magazine is often described as "what *Mother Earth* used to be." It is low-tech, anything but glossy, and probably the best single source of self-sufficient living information from people who've *been there*. It contains practical advice on: raising animals and growing vegetables; building inexpensive homes; using your computer to earn a living in an isolated area; controlling four-legged varmints; using solar, wind, water and generator power; canning; cooking; home-schooling and living cheaply. You'll also find a regular firearms column by self-defense expert Massad Ayoob, articles that help you look at "common knowledge" from an uncommon perspective, and editorials expressing an independent conservative-libertarian philosophy. *Backwoods Home* also reviews and sells many books on self-sufficiency, and contains the most helpful ads in the world.

For a subscription, or information contact:
Backwoods Home Magazine
P.O. Box 40
Montague, California 96064
voice: (916) 459-3300
credit card orders only: 1-800-835-2418
e-mail: editor@backwoodshome.com
Web site: http://www.backwoodshome.com

Putting Food By, by Ruth Hertzberg, Beatrice Vaughan and Janet Greene, Penguin USA, 1992. This classic, oft-revised, oft-reprinted book by a home economics teacher, a cookbook author and an expert on Americana tells simply everything you need to know about preserving foods.

Your Money or Your Life, by Joe Dominguez and Vicki Robin, Viking, New York, 1992. This book will not only teach you how to live inexpensively; it will teach you to think about money in an entirely new, and very healthy, way. Its goal is to enable *anyone* to live without a job, spending your time as you wish. A truly revolutionary book — and a practical one by people who live the life they write about.

Starting Over, by Robert L. Williams, WRS, Waco, Texas, 1993. (Available by mail from *Backwoods Home*.) If you are changing your lifestyle — or if your lifestyle has suddenly been changed for you by a natural or man-made disaster — this book can help you get re-established, both emotionally and physically.

Carla Emery's Encyclopedia of Country Living, Sasquatch Books, Seattle, 1994. This great project began more than 20 years ago as a mimeographed self-publication produced in fits, starts and segments by an overworked and slightly obsessed Idaho farmwife. It has evolved into an institution of country living. You might find early editions under the title *Carla Emery's Old Fashioned Recipe Book*, but it never was and never will be just a cookbook. Want to know how to butcher a hog, keep bees, conserve water, bake bread, cook brains and tongue, milk goats, hitch cattle to a plow, treat poisonous bites and buy cheaply at auction? It's all here.

Directions: Information for the Prepared Citizen (newsletter). This low-budget newsletter contains information on various survival techniques, from survival gardening and storing water to purchasing and caching appropriate weapons. *Directions* is published by: Live Free International, 11123 S. St. Lawrence Avenue, Chicago, IL 60628, (312) 821-LIVE. If you saw *Directions* within the last few years and weren't impressed, give it another look; new editors have brought the focus back to real survival issues.

Vonu: The Search for Personal Freedom, by Rayo, edited by Jon Fisher, Loompanics Unlimited, 1983. This collection of articles was written by a practical idealist who lived a primitive existence in the woods, wrote advice about it and philosophized about it. The lifestyle he experimented with — living out of cars or in makeshift shelters — isn't something most of us would want to try for long. But in an emergency, or as a protest against the powers-that-be, Rayo's ideas could come in handy. (Vonu means "invulnerability to coercion." Invisibility to authority is a large component of it.)

Travel-Trailer Homesteading Under $5,000, by Brian Kelling, Loompanics Unlimited, 1995. This little 65-page book tells you how to find your trailer and your land, choose and install solar panels, build your own septic system, install a wood stove, deal with nosy county bureaucrats and live successfully in a trailer. The author — whose own trailer/home is shown on the cover, shares both his mistakes and his successes. Very simple, yet very inspiring, knowing you can actually have a home for less than $5,000.

The Loompanics catalog contains sections titled "Survival," "Self-Sufficiency," "Head for the Hills," and "Gimme Shelter." These list books on everything from barter techniques to poaching to solar power to finding freedom on the road.

Read anything by Bradford Angier, backwoods survival expert.

49. Read: strategic thinking and fighting
The first five books on the list are all available from Loompanics Unlimited:

- *To Break a Tyrant's Chains: Neo-Guerrilla Techniques for Combat*, by Duncan Long, 1991.
- *Coup d'Etat: A Practical Handbook*, by Edward Luttwak
- *Disruptive Terrorism*, by Victor Santoro

- *Black Books, Volumes 1 & 2 (Improvised Munitions Handbook)*
- *Home Workshop Explosives*, by Uncle Fester

A Helpful Hint from Hell-Louise: Avoid *The Anarchist's Cookbook*. Chemically wise people say this famous guide to explosives should have been titled *The Amateur's Cookbook*. These same people say Uncle Fester's book is the real thing. (I can barely mix a cup of hot chocolate without blowing up my kitchen, so don't trust me. Check it with a chemist friend of your own.)

Books from other publishers:

Mao's Road to Power: Revolutionary Writings 1912-1949, by Mao Tse-Tung, M.E. Sharpe. This three-volume set is too horrendously expensive to buy, but if you can get it at a university library or public library, you might want to look up some of "Chairman Mao's" observations on revolutionary strategy. For a more accessible version of Mao's views and tactics try:

Mao Tse-Tung on Guerrilla Warfare, Samuel B. Griffith II, Nautical and Aviation Publishing Company of America, 1991.

Guerilla Warfare, Che Guevara, University of Nebraska Press, 1985. More advice from someone who did it in the real world.

From the Barrel of a Gun: A History of Guerrilla, Revolutionary and Counter-Insurgency Warfare from the Romans to the Present, John Ellis, Stackpole Books, 1995. The title says it all.

Armed People Victorious, Larry Pratt, Gun Owners Foundation, 1990.

U.S. Army manuals. Some of the best advice on explosives, military firearms, tactics and emergency survival comes, quite unintentionally, from the U.S. Army. (Thank you, Uncle Sam!) This is not only tried & true advice (unlike some of the untested fantasies that come from some publishers of militaria) but it's written in very simple, impossible to screw up language. Look for Army manuals at almost any sizable gun show, surplus store, or survival goods store. They are usually over-distributed to military bases, and the Army does not discourage civilians from getting many of them. A friend in the Army or National Guard might be able to give you some, or you could simply walk into a National Guard armory and ask for the less controversial ones. Some good, fundamental information can be found in: *The Soldier's Manual of Common Tasks, Skill Level 1* (STP-21-1-SMCT — for enlisted people*), The Soldier's Manual of Common Tasks, Skill Levels 2-4* (STP-21-24-SMCT — for their supervisors and trainers) and *Survival* (FM 21-76). The latter is a kind of Boy Scout manual for adults, with information on survival medicine, direction finding, signaling, camouflage, contacts with local people in possibly hostile areas, edible plants, poisonous plants, finding water, lighting fires, dangerous animals, and survival under various weather conditions. It comes complete with great photographs of plants and critters. More specialized manuals, such as those on explosives and weapons, aren't as readily available, but check those gun shows.

Total Resistance: The Swiss Army Guide to Guerrilla Warfare and Underground Operations, by Major H. von Dach Bern, Paladin Press, Boulder, Colorado. Living in the incipient American police state, it's hard to believe that there is actually a country that encourages individuals to arm themselves and learn resistance movement techniques, but little Switzerland does. *Total Resistance* is the classic guide to organizing a resistance movement, caching weapons, blowing up train tracks and taking down power lines. Some of the advice is dated now. (There are, for instance, much more modern ways to cache weapons, detailed in *Bury gold, guns and goodies,* No. 97.) But the book is worth it merely for its excellent background on the philosophy and organization of resistance.

Other books from Paladin Press. The Paladin mail order catalog includes several hundred books in the following categories: weapons, combat shooting, financial freedom, new ID and personal freedom, silencers, sniping, knives & knife fighting, special forces, police science, espionage and investigation, martial arts, self-defense, locksmithing, terrorism, revenge and humor, military science, action careers, and explosives and demolition.

Request a catalog from:
Paladin Press
P.O. Box 1307
Boulder, Colorado 80306
voice: (303) 443-7250
fax: (303) 442-8741
e-mail: pala@rmii.com
Web site: http://www.paladin-press.com/
Some of the books in the Paladin catalog are actually published by Loompanics, so (says the voice of author loyalty), check *The Best Book Catalog in the World* first.

You Are Going to Prison, by Jim Hogshire, Loompanics Unlimited, 1994. I debated about whether this book belonged under the category of "strategic thinking." But where else? Every strategic plan should include preparations for the worst case — and going to prison, as Hogshire describes it, could be worse than death. Hogshire, who knows what he's talking about, tells what to expect and how best to cope. He gives hard, no-nonsense, no-holds-barred details on everything from arrest and preliminary hearings through life in prison and execution. Be prepared. In a police state, the best of people go to prison.

50. Read: political periodicals

Liberty
P.O. Box 1187
Port Townsend, Washington 98368
Web site: http://libertysoft.com/liberty/liberty.html

Liberty is a bi-monthly whose publisher describes it as "a libertarian and classical liberal review of thought, culture and politics." It regularly features many pages of brief, often funny commentary by its hordes of regular contributors. It contains longer articles such as "A Short and Absurd History of Schooling" and "Dopers in the Hands of an Angry God" (about Puritanism in the drug war). Quality of individual articles is up and down, with a few contributors trying to out-intellectualize God and others writing at a level even I can understand. Viewpoints are all over the place, which is fun, as various contributors beat on each other's opinions. Very stimulating reading.

Reason
3415 S. Sepulveda Blvd., Suite 400
Los Angeles, California 90034-6064
voice: 1-800-403-6397
fax: (310) 391-4395
Web site: http://www.reasonmag.com/
E-mail: reason@enews.com

There was a time I thought I'd never be without a sub-scription to *Reason*. Now it bores me. It represents the main-stream of mainstream libertarian thinking (if there is such a thing). Though its motto is "Free minds and free markets," it emphasizes the "markets" part as if it wishes all that untidy "free minds" stuff would go away. Some months it strikes me as more conservative than libertarian. Nevertheless, I list it here because it is still a solid, real-world issue-oriented publication, and it might be just the thing for bringing your stodgy Republican friends closer to libertarianism.

The Freeman
The Foundation for Economic Education
30 South Broadway
Irvington-on-Hudson, New York 10533
voice: (914) 591-7230, subscription number: 1-800-452-3518
fax: (914) 591-8910
Web site: http://www.self-gov.org/freeman

The Freeman has been around forever. It is nice, non-confrontational libertarianism, very good for educating people confused about freedom issues.

Modern Militiaman
c/o Martin Lindstedt, R.I.
338 Rabbit Track Road
Granby, Missouri 64844
e-mail: mlindste@mo-net.com or mlindste@clandjop.com
Web site: http://www.mo-net.com/~mlindste/index.html
or http://www.clandjop.com/~mlindste/index.html

Modern Militiaman is an electronic publication, filled with practical, well-written (and often witty) information for people in the freedom movement. Its articles cover much of the same type of information given in *101 Things to Do 'til the Revolution*, but in greater depth, and with the militia community in mind. It's free on the Internet, $5.00 per copy on diskette.

Media Bypass
4900 Tippecanoe
Evansville, Indiana 47715
order number: 1-800-4bypass
fax: 812-477-8677
e-mail: subscribe@4bypass.com
Web site: http://www.4bypass.com
Deliberately adopting the "look" of a *Time* or *Newsweek*, these guys bill themselves as "The uncensored national news." Well, maybe, but they are an interesting alternative to the mainstream news magazines.

The Nation
P.O. Box 37072
Boone, Iowa 50037
1-800-333-2536
e-mail: info@thenation.com
Web site: http://thenation.com
These guys are on a very different corner of the political spectrum than most readers of this book. I include *The Nation* here for two reasons: 1) It's always useful to see what the opposition is thinking; and, 2) publishers of *The Nation* represent an old segment of the left that we might wish to see standing strong in this country once again. Whatever their economic views, they have a high regard for civil liberties and a horror at watching our rights be legislated away to a police state. (The address given is for subscriptions only. Editorial offices are in New York City.)

Covert Action Quarterly
c/o InfoMed On-Line Services
PO Box 5050
Philadelphia, PA 19111
Web site: http://www.w2.com/docs2/covertaction.html

Like *The Nation,* this is what you might call a "far left" publication if you were fond of attaching labels to things. (Oh well, sometimes I am.) And like *The Nation*, it strongly supports civil rights and decries their erosion. *CAQ,* however, has an entirely different, and fascinating focus; it reports on activities of the CIA, NSA and other secretive government bureaus, in the U.S. and throughout the world. You will definitely read things here you won't find in any other publication. At least, you won't find them in any mainstream publication until long after *CAQ* has broken the story.

Very big-time important note about books that can help you learn to perform un-approved activities:

Don't get them from the library!!!

Libraries are wonderful places — mostly. But they have become rotten places to get information that provokes government paranoia. Under a quiet little FBI scheme called the Library Assistance Program, that mousy lady or man behind the counter is now encouraged to report anyone who requests "suspicious" books.

No kidding, people. Things have gotten that bad. Your hometown librarian is a fedgov fink.

"Suspicious" items can include something as innocuous as a chemistry textbook. (That nasty chemistry stuff is what makes drugs or explosives; I'm surprised Congress hasn't banned the whole science!) It's entirely up to the librarian to decide what might be subversive or criminal reading habits.

Certainly you're pointing a finger at yourself if you check out anything like *The Anarchist's Cookbook*. But the sad fact is, you can never be sure what might trigger some librarian's little James Bond fantasy. Be cautious.

51. You can't kill the beast while sucking at its teat

You cannot untie yourself from the apron strings of the nanny state while scarfing up nanny's goodies. Do not accept: food stamps, welfare, housing allowances, Medicaid, Social Security benefits, government jobs, independent government contracts, business subsidies or any other government handout, privilege or special consideration.

You say you've paid for all this with your taxes? Then stop paying! But don't take other people's money under the thin justification that it's really your money coming back to you. That's just the story we hand ourselves to ease our conscience and justify "doing unto others as they do unto us."

Nobody can liberate him or herself entirely from the government. We can't avoid driving on its roads or using its post office. Even if we try to live in a tree or a cave, that tree or cave is either on taxed property or tax-exempt (subsidized) property, but you *can* avoid actively and deliberately making yourself part of the problem.

A Democracy cannot exist as a permanent form of government. It can exist only until the voters discover that they can vote themselves largesse from the public treasury. From that moment on, the majority always votes for the candidates promising the most benefits from the public treasury, with the result that a

Democracy always collapses over loose fiscal policy, always followed by dictatorship.

The average age of the world's greatest civilizations has been two hundred years. These nations have progressed through this sequence: From bondage to spiritual faith; from spiritual faith to great courage; from courage to liberty; from liberty to abundance; from abundance to selfishness; from selfishness to complacency; from complacency to apathy; from apathy to dependence; from dependency back again into bondage.

— by Fraser Tyler, English historian — Written while the U.S. was still a British colony

52. On the other hand...

I can think of two possible exceptions to the idea that you should avoid taking anything from government.

One: If you decide to bring down the system...or if the system has already brought you down through political persecution, incarceration or confiscation of everything you own...then one way to make sure the system falls faster is to suck it dry.

If the IRS says, "Give us everything you own," you might be perfectly justified in saying, "Okay, if you're determined to punish me for being productive, I'll stop producing. I've just become a professional leech." Then go out and apply for every form of government handout available to you.

But if you decide to try to bring the system down by taking advantage of its benefits, keep two things in mind: 1) you might just be kidding yourself and taking the easy way out — a hypocrite; and, 2) once you do bring it down, how are you going to survive without its benefits?

You're probably better off keeping your independence, even if it means living by dumpster diving (See *Learn Dumpster diving,* No. 72) or holing up in a travel trailer home (See *Read: self-reliance,* No. 48).

Two: If you're in a government job where you can do some "good" you might ease some pain and slow the march of tyranny by staying there. I once knew a man, for instance, who allowed himself to be appointed to the state education commission with the goal of abolishing the government school system. Maybe there's some justification for that, or for being a city councilperson defending property rights, a cop fairly enforcing laws, a soldier upholding his or her oath to defend the Constitution or some such.

I'm not sure, though. It's a difficult question, and individuals must answer it for themselves. But realistically, can police officers refuse to enforce unjust laws? How many soldiers dare stand up and say, "I won't fight under UN authority" or "I won't let myself be used in illegal actions against American citizens"? Besides, the entire premise of this book is that it's too late to "change the system" from inside or out. One of the surest ways to help the system fall is for all the good people to leave it. Instead of hanging around government and trying to help minimize its damage, you'd be better off putting your intelligence to work maximizing freedom.

> *A government that is big enough to give you all you want is big enough to take it all away.*
> — Barry Goldwater

53. Bust anti-freedom organizations by driving them broke

Remember the "death clock"? It went up in Times Square amid much media hoopla. Though it was nothing but a mechanical device that ticked over every so often and tossed up a new number, its sponsor, Robert Brennan of Dehere Gunfighters, claimed it showed how many people were being killed every year by those evil (and apparently self-firing) guns. The national media was soon reporting the clock's made-up numbers as the official U.S. firearm death count.

Do you remember that the clock quietly died without a mention in the press? It was killed within the year. Gun owners blew it away using a "bullet" provided by Mr. Brennan himself. The bullet was Dehere's 1-800 number.

Gun owners called and called and called and called and called. They posted the number on computer bulletin boards and passed it around to their friends, who called and called and called and called and called. With each call costing Brennan around 85¢ and yielding no donations, Dehere and its clock quickly expired.

The delicious irony of the "death clock's" demise is that Robert Brennan was actually a crook who had scammed investors in his securities firm out of millions of dollars. He was even part owner of a shooting range! He'd simply planned to use the clock to suck dollars out of soft-hearted fools who, he figured, would use the 800 number to dial in donations.

You can help kill — or at least damage — "legitimate" anti-freedom organizations the same way that illegitimate outfit was bumped off.

If the organization has an 800 number, call, distribute the number widely, and ask your friends to call. But keep these techniques in mind:

- Never dial more than once or twice from your home or office number. Many organizations have now gotten wise and installed systems that block the third or fourth call from the same number. Besides which, repeated calls can be considered harassment.

- To get around call blocks or harassment charges, go to a public place like an airport or a college campus where you find banks of pay phones. Move from one phone to another, calling, calling and calling.

- Call every time you're out at a shopping mall or grocery store.

- Don't just call and hang up every time, or blurt, "Sorry, wrong number." Ask the organization to send you its literature. Ask them to send literature to your mother, your father, your aunt, your sister in Tucson, your brother in Nome, your best friend, your next-door neighbor and your third cousin's dog Max. Every packet they send costs them money.

- If you receive a literature packet with a postage-paid envelope inside, mail it back. That costs them money, too. (It's tempting either to stuff all the literature in the envelope to make it weigh more, or to attach the envelope to a brick, but that's pretty easy to spot and they might simply refuse delivery.)

Even if the organization has no 800 number, you can still cost them money by requesting their literature. Some of these outfits send glossy packets that appear to cost several dollars. As long as they keep you on their mailing lists, you're helping shove them down the financial tubes.

Only drawback is, some organizations are so desperate to inflate their membership to the media they claim every person on their mailing list is a "member." So you might find yourself in the aggravating position of being a "member" of the League to Save the Endangered Anopheles Mosquito from Abortion by Handgun Violence. Oh, well.

The government is mainly an expensive organization to regulate evildoers and tax those who behave; government does little for fairly respectable people except annoy them.
— E.W. Howe, 1926

54. Another charming use for 1-800 numbers

Report a statist. Did you know anyone can anonymously call the IRS to report that a friend, family member, acquaintance — or absolute stranger — might be evading taxes? The IRS will investigate, too, and you know what a pleasant experience that is.

Lots of police agencies have these lines. Lots of governments have so-called "waste, fraud and abuse" lines to let you report all kinds of wrongdoing.

Well, isn't violating the Bill of Rights "wrongdoing"? Isn't stealing people's property under color of law "wrongdoing"? Isn't interfering with your consensual activities "wrongdoing"? Isn't running a protection racket (e.g. tax system) "wrongdoing"? Isn't running a Ponzi scheme (e.g. Social Security) "wrongdoing"?

If some anonymous joker can sic goons on you without cause, well, do unto others. Especially, do unto the very people who think taxes, anonymous informants, and various other outrages are such a damned good idea.

Never do it just for personal spite. That neighbor whose dog barks all day doesn't deserve this, no matter how much you hate him. But as a political tool...

Here are a few national sources to get you started. Local police agencies also undoubtedly have anonymous tips lines you can add to this list. So do many state agencies. If numbers have changed by the time you read this, check your library, an on-line directory of 1-800 numbers, or a CD-ROM containing phone numbers from around the U.S.

Where there is no national hotline, you can get the number of an agency's nearest regional office from the Federal Information Center at 1-800-688-9889.

U.S. Customs Drug Smuggling Hotline	1-800-232-5378
U.S. Navy Espionage Hotline	1-800-543-6289
Resolution Trust Corporation Fraud Hotline	1-800-833-3310
U.S. Inspector General's Hotline for Fraud, Waste & Abuse	1-800-424-4000
IRS Hotline	1-800-829-1040
Drug Enforcement Administration	No hotline: call your regional field office.
U.S. Marshals Service	No hotline: call your regional field office.
Bureau of Alcohol, Tobacco and Firearms (A list of BATF office numbers can be found at hhtp://www.aft.treas.gov/@_ATF/PHONE/phone.html	No hotline: call your regional field office.
Federal Bureau of Investigation	No hotline; call your regional field office; there are 56 in the U.S., as well as hundreds of local offices.

IMPORTANT NOTE: Never, never, never make these calls from your home or office. Not even from the home or office of a friend. Not even if you are using a pre-paid phone card for privacy. "Anonymous" or not, your call is traceable.

Phone booths only, please! Or call (without his or her knowledge) from the home or office of someone you detest.

55. Respect the individual, not the office

Some say we should respect the office — like that of the presidency — even if we don't respect the individual in it. Bullshit. The office doesn't exist aside from the individual. The office is only as worthy as the lowest oaf who plants his or her ass on its chair. Bill Clinton. Richard Nixon. That's what the "glory" of the presidency is worth. Give no person, no office and no institution unearned respect.

It is easy for strength to acquire a reputation, but not for reputation to acquire strength.
— Niccolò Machiavelli

56. Don't blame anybody else for your troubles

Unless someone is holding a gun to your head, your life and your decisions belong to you. Take the responsibility. Hell, even if you're held at gun point you still have the option of saying, "Screw you!" and taking the consequences.

But let's say your ex-girlfriend *did* jerk you around, or your parents *didn't* love you, or your boss *won't* give you a break — so what? Do you prefer to sit around and whine about it or are you going to get on with things — and *live*?

The victim mentality has become endemic to our culture. Understandable. Being a certified, politically approved victim gives you more political clout than almost anything else. The whole idea of "entitlements" was built around the idea that victimhood and helplessness give thee a moral and monetary claim on me.

I say, "No way!"

57. Stand up for people who stand up for their rights

Remember Michael New, the medic who refused to wear a U.N. uniform? Remember Al Woodbridge, sent to federal prison because he dared defy the BATF? Remember the marijuana activists who publicly planted hemp seeds in defiance of the law? Remember juror Laura Kriho who was hit with vengeful criminal charges after she voted her conscience instead of blindly following a judge's orders?

Did you send any money to their defense funds? Did you volunteer labor to their cause? Did you write a letter to a newspaper or magazine on their behalf? Did you contribute to an organization pledged to help them? Did you distribute articles about their dilemma?

If not, why not?

If you're not willing to stand up for people who stand up for what they believe in, who's going to stand up for you when the time comes?

You can't help everybody. There are too many injustices, and more being perpetrated all the time, but pick one or two gutsy individuals a year and give them the best you can.

> *Whoever lays a hand on me to govern me is a usurper and a tyrant, and I declare him my enemy.*
> — P.J. Proudhon

58. Don't cooperate with the friendly census taker

Here's a painless little way you can stand up for your own rights in defiance of the law.

The Constitution allows the federal government to take a census every 10 years. The census has one lawful purpose, and one only — to determine how many people live in a given area so congressional districts can be divided up relatively equally.

So when that census form arrives in your mail, give the feds precisely the information they are legally entitled to: one, two, three, four or whatever number of people live in your house.

Don't tell them your marital status, your race, the ages of your family members, the number of telephones or TV sets or commodes you have in your house — or anything else. It isn't their business, and they are exceeding their legal authority in asking.

Theoretically, there are penalties for refusing. Have you ever heard of anyone being prosecuted or fined for telling a census taker go to hell?

Only once did the Census Bureau ever send a man to my door to request the remaining information. I told him no and told him why. The only consequence I experienced was that he thanked me for refusing him more politely than all the other refusers, then went away.

If you're an anarchist, of course, you might just want to tear up the form altogether. Or lie. They won't know what to do if you tell them you're a Jewish Pacific islander of African descent living in a one bedroom house with six wives, three co-husbands, 300 television sets and a donkey.

The smallest and most inoffensive state is still criminal in its dreams.
— Michael Bakunin, Russian anarchist

59. Know where your line in the sand is drawn

What are the things that you will not tolerate? What is the point beyond which you will not be pushed? What is the injustice that will cause you to fling yourself into the claws of the fiercest adversary, ready to fight?

On the other hand, what annoyances are not worth the energy to oppose them?

Know these things. Avoid getting hyped up over things that really don't count. Take a deep breath and save your body and mind for the big stuff, but know what your personal "big stuff" is.

Know where your line is drawn. Cast it in concrete. Then let the world know: This is the point past which no one dares tread.

A different view: My friend Kevin, who read the first draft of this manuscript, said, "I completely disagree with this point."

Why?

"Because my line in the sand is already drawn right in front of these shoes. When it comes to government stealing my rights, I won't tolerate anything more. That time is over."

That's the way mild-tempered, middle class guys are feeling these days. Encouraging, isn't it?

> *The spirit of resistance to government is so valuable*
> *on certain occasions, that I wish it to be always kept*
> *alive. It will often be exercised when wrong, but better*
> *so than not to be exercised at all. I like a little*
> *rebellion now and then. It is like a storm in the*
> *atmosphere.*
>
> — Thomas Jefferson, letter to Abigail Adams

60. Buy and carry the Citizens' Rule Book

This one's not for the anarchists among us, although "practical anarchists" — willing to take the long road through minarchism first — might find it useful.

There's a little book you'll see in the pockets of members of the Patriot movement. It's called the Citizens' Rule Book and it contains the Declaration of Independence, Constitution and Bill of Rights, and information on the rights and responsibilities of jurors.

It's a handy-dandy little reference. Could be useful in a discussion or if a cop stops you. ("Where's your concealed carry permit?" "Right here, officer. See? Amendment Article II." "May I look in the trunk of your car?" "No, sir. It says here in Amendment Article IV...")

These little books are inexpensive, and even more so when purchased in quantity. You can buy them from a number of sources including:

Militia of Montana
P.O. Box 1486
Noxon, Montana 59853
voice: (406) 847-2735
fax: (406) 847-2246
e-mail: mom@logoplex.com
Web site: http://www.logoplex.com/shops/mom/

If you are interested in consitutional issues including history, Supreme Court judgments, organizations, publications, check out the Constitution Society's outstanding Web site at http://www.constitution.org. The page also contains leads to government sources, publishers, freedom-oriented publications and a wealth of other useful organizations and information.

"I have no defense."

"Do you —" the judge stumbled... "Do you throw yourself upon the mercy of this court?"

"I do not recognize this court's right to try me."

"But Mr. Rearden, this is the legally appointed court to try this particular category of crime."

"I do not recognize my action as a crime."

"But you have admitted you have broken our regulations concerning the sale of your Metal."

"I do not recognize your right to control the sale of my Metal."

"Is it necessary for me to point out that your recognition was not required?"

"No. I am fully aware of it and I am acting accordingly."

... "Do you mean that you are refusing to obey the law?" asked the judge.

"No, I am complying with the law — to the letter. Your law holds that my life, my work and my property may be disposed of without my consent. Very well, you may now dispose of me without my participation in the matter. I will not play the part of defending myself, where no defense is possible, and I will not simulate the illusion of dealing with a tribunal of justice."

— Ayn Rand, *Atlas Shrugged*

61. Join FIJA

FIJA is the Fully Informed Jury Association. It has one clear, simple, beautiful purpose: to tell jurors and prospective jurors what modern judges will not—that they have the right to judge the law as well as the facts.

If you're on a jury and you think a law is stupid or unfair, you have every right to find the defendant not guilty on that basis. It's an ancient right, and it's one juries have often exercised by default anyway. (One reason prohibition ended was that juries were refusing to convict people who violated it. Today some juries are beginning to use it in tax cases and minor drug cases. Three juries used it in their refusals to convict Jack Kevorkian.) But judges — with no basis in law or tradition — usually tell jurors the exact opposite.

U.S. law was never meant to be something imposed on citizens against their will. Neither was the Supreme Court ever given sole authority to decide if a law is right or wrong. (They gave *themselves* that authority in *Marbury v. Madison*, an early 19th century case!)

The *people* have the right to determine if laws are fair or unfair: Always have; Always will. FIJA volunteers give literature to jurors and trial-goers to remind them of that fact — even though they risk "jury tampering" charges to do so.

FIJA deserves everyone's support.

Fully Informed Jury Association
P.O. Box 59
Helmville, Montana 59843
1-800-TEL-JURY
Web page: http://www.primenet.com/~slack/fija/fija.html

Is life so dear, or peace so sweet as to be purchased at the price of chains and slavery? Forbid it, Almighty God! I know not what course others may take, but as for me, give me Liberty or give me death!
— Patrick Henry

62. Keep a record of your dreams

When you're going through a time of change or having a hard time making an important decision, heed your dreams.

No, I'm not going mystical or New Age here. Your dreams are simply your unconscious mind talking to you. That hidden layer of your self often hears, sees and understands things your busy, data-filled consciousness misses.

Write your dreams down. It's in the act of writing that you can best grasp their meaning, and it's certainly in the writing that you'll recognize patterns over time. Even though any given dream may never make sense, in the long run, your sleeping mind can help you discover the inspiration and knowledge you need to move ahead, make that decision, or get over that crisis.

63. Consider sovereign citizenship

Sovereigns declare their independence from the U.S. federal government and, in some cases, from state governments as well.

They make not merely an emotional or intellectual declaration, but a legal one. Sovereigns rescind their Social Security numbers, refuse to license vehicles with the state, will not accept state drivers licenses, do not pay certain taxes, and otherwise separate themselves from the government.

Sovereignty is a very, very complex subject. Personally, although I think most sovereigns have their heart in the right place, I'm dubious of their methods. Also, sovereigns — attuned to detailed, legalistic wrangling — tend to jump on anyone who misrepresents their movement in the slightest way. I don't personally use or endorse these techniques.

For those reasons, I'll let the sovereigns themselves tell you more about their philosophy and methods. Check them out via these and other sources:

Freedom & Sovereign Technology
Kedar R. Cohen
5595 East 7th Street, #229
Long Beach, California [90804]
voice: 562-436-9604

e-mail: krcohen@hotmail.com
Web site: http://www.telesouth1.com/~krcohen/fasthime.htm

Sovereign Rights Forum

e-mail: sovereignright@geocities.com
Web site: http://www.geocities.com/CapitolHill/2917

The Sovereign Christian Resource Center
voice: 520-348-9864

e-mail: scrc@cogent.net
Web page: http://www.cogent.net/scrc

Among other things, The Sovereign Christian Resource Center sells foreign license plates, passports, instructions on how to not pay taxes, forms for filing various actions, and so on.

Note: Some sovereigns reject both zip codes and two-letter state postal codes.

Essays about sovereignty can be found on the World Wide Web at:

http://users.aol.com/dritus/private/links/cases.htm

You can also participate in the *alt.society.sovereign* Internet news group, or subscribe to a patriot's discussion group by sending e-mail to listserv@kaiwan.com and typing the words "subscribe patriots" in the body of your message.

One caution: There are a number of organizations "selling" packaged sovereignty services for fees in the $5,000 range and up. They claim they'll do all the paperwork and run interference with the government for you. When you ask precisely what services they provide, and with what guarantees, they get huffy, as if you've just asked the Queen of England if her hemorrhoids are bothering her today. This "how dare you question me" attitude is typical of scam artists (and, for that matter, government employees — Or am I being redundant?). Be careful! There are many sincere and successful sovereigns, but the movement tends to attract true believers, and thus has its share of both frauds and fools. If anyone demands more information from you than they're willing to give about themselves you can be certain they're either scammers or government agents.

The ultimate consequence of protecting men from the results of their own folly is to fill the world with fools.

— Herbert Spencer

64. Get your records to safety

When preparing for disasters, one thing we often forget is to take care of our paperwork — auto titles, deeds, passports, birth certificates, insurance papers and that sort of thing.

Putting it all in a safe deposit box is okay most of the time; a bank vault is better at surviving fire, flood, earthquake and attempted theft than your dresser drawer. But putting your passport in there could cause problems; what if you have to make an emergency trip out of the country on a Sunday?

And putting *anything* there will be a problem if the police are after you; they can seize your safe deposit box in a heartbeat.

You might consider putting documents underground. Unlike guns, you could even stash them on your own property. A plastic tube filled with papers is less detectable than one with metal. (But in that case, use some of the same protections against moisture you used with your weapons. See *Bury gold, guns and goodies*, No. 97).

Other methods of hiding are detailed in *How to Hide Anything*, by Michael Connor, *The Big Book of Secret Hiding Places*, by Jack Luger, and *How to Hide Things In Public Places*, by Dennis Fiery, all available from Loompanics. Just be sure the method you choose protects against fire and natural disaster, as well as freelance or government theft. Keep in mind both increasingly sophisticated snooping technologies, like infrared sensors and miniature fiber-optic cameras, and the growing likelihood of property seizure.

In some urban areas, companies offer private safe deposit boxes you can rent with more confidentiality than a box at the bank. Pay the rent in cash, and preferably under another name.

Don't forget your Rolodex!

Whatever else you do, don't forget this: your address book, Rolodex or address database is right up there with the most valuable records you own. If you're thrown off your property, or if everything you own is snatched, how else will you contact people who can help?

You should always keep a current copy of your address list safely hidden. If it contains names of people the police might harass — like members of your militia group, your customers, or your suppliers of recreational substances — for God's sake encrypt it or otherwise make sure the goons won't be able to read it if it falls into their hands.

65. Watch your local government

The mayors of two little towns near me both refer to federal and state grants as "free money" and brag about using it to put up statues and landscape Main Street.

I was at a city council meeting where one member resigned and, by pre-arrangement among the cronies, the mayor had a friend right there, ready to appoint in his place, without any nominations or public hearings as the law required.

Washington, DC isn't the only place in the universe where corrupt, pork barreling politicians hold sway. It's a characteristic of the breed. These people start with the assumption that they're entitled to run your life, that taxes are good, that "quality of life" involves spending millions on parks that might just get named after them. Then their behavior goes downhill from there.

In fact, these guys often get away with worse corruption and spending than the people in Washington. They aren't watched as closely.

So watch them. Get together with a group of citizens and make sure one of you always attends every city council, county commission, school board and zoning commission meeting. Ask questions. Look up laws and ordinances. Call the local newspaper editor's attention to dubious doings. Howl like a banshee. Make their lives living hell. They may still get away with corruption, but not without having to blast through your wall of opposition.

Join or forge alliances with other local groups that fight this sort of thing, too.

You *can* fight city hall. It's more gratifying than fighting Washington, because despite the old saying, you have a better chance of winning at this level.

How does it become a man to behave toward this American government today? I answer, that he cannot without disgrace be associated with it.
— Henry David Thoreau

66. Don't let your possessions imprison you

Your belongings can imprison you in a lot of ways.

One, buying nice cars, stereos, spas, boats, houses and such can keep you in permanent debt bondage, so you never have the freedom to quit your job, take more time for yourself, relax and tell society to go to hell.

Two, you can get hung up on owning things for the sake of things. I mean, on the day you die, is it going to make any difference whether you owned a Lexus or a Geo? Whether your CD player had a sixty disk changer or a six disk changer?

Three, you can get so attached to them that, if they're stolen or destroyed in a fire, you suffer more than you should.

Four, they can literally imprison you if a crooked police agency, drooling with desire for property seizure, covets what you own enough to trump up evidence of a crime.

At the very least, keep your expensive goodies hidden from the world. Never brag and flaunt 'em.

Better yet, consider dumping them. Or pay off the ones you have and don't tempt yourself with more. There are better things in life than owning a jet boat or a three-carat diamond ring. Not just more important things — but literally things you'll like better once you get in the habit.

67. Cultivate cheap tastes

Here are some of those things you might ultimately find more satisfying than devoting your life to expensive toys:

- Long evenings of sensuousness with your partner.
- Wading in a lake or the ocean.
- Tubing on a river.
- Playing cards.
- Reading.

- An evening of great conversation with friends.
- Attending a free concert in a park.
- Playing games with your kids.
- Walking the dog.
- Picnicking in a lonely meadow.
- Learning a survival skill.
- Writing a book.
- Baking bread.
- Making your own clothes.
- Attending free lectures at the library.
- Shooting your .22 at cans in the local quarry.
- Joining a softball league.
- Learning embroidery or woodworking.
- Building your own house out of scrounged materials.
- Planting a veggie garden.
- Collecting wild flowers.
- Reading with your kids.
- Giving and getting massages from your partner.
- Hosting pot-luck dinners.
- Hiking.
- Shopping at flea markets.
- Selling at flea markets.
- Raising chickens.
- Starting a home business.
- Playing basketball with neighbors in your driveway.
- Drawing or painting.
- Attending political gatherings.
- Helping a friend restore an old car. (But your friend pays the bills!)
- Rebuilding and selling antique furniture or radios.
- Sitting on your front porch or deck on a summer evening.
- Building a raft.

- Playing chess.
- Running a 10k race.
- Going for a swim.
- A thousand more things you can think of.

It doesn't take money to have fun and someday you may need to have fun without money. Best to start now.

If you love wealth greater than liberty, the tranquillity of servitude greater than the animating contest of freedom, go home from us in peace. We seek not your counsel, nor your arms. Crouch down and lick the hand that feeds you. May your chains set lightly upon you; and may posterity forget that you were our countrymen.
— Samuel Adams, American Revolutionary

68. Close your bank accounts

Did you know that, under the Clinton Terrorism law, your banker is authorized to freeze your accounts and report you to the feds if they suspect you of "terrorism"?

They don't have to have a warrant. Not even any legal evidence. If you've done something as innocuous as writing a check to an organization your banker thinks is suspicious, zap!

Your bank is not only authorized to do it; they're encouraged. Banks that fail to guess when customers are using their accounts for "terrorism" can get clobbered with fines and prosecution.

This is just one of a long line of abuses which, since the 1970s, has converted your banker into a federal informant. A relationship that ought to be as confidential as the one between you and your lawyer or priest is now nothing but a

trap. You supply the information on yourself and your banker gives it to the feds. The statement they send to the IRS every year on each of your interest-bearing accounts is violation enough, but it's getting way worse than that.
So:

- If possible, close all U.S. bank accounts. How to cope after that? Ask if your employer or clients will pay in cash. If not, cash your paychecks at your employer's bank, a local Western Union office or other private check-cashing service; fees are high at these private businesses (2½ to 3 percent of the check), but the businesses do less finking than your bank.[1] Use cash or money orders for most purchases.

- If you absolutely must have a U.S. bank account, open a non-interest-bearing checking account and refuse to give your Social Security number. The bank cannot legally refuse you. (Only when there's interest involved can they demand your Social Security number.) Non-interest-bearing accounts do not have to be reported to the IRS.

- Even if you keep a bank account, don't write checks to political organizations or other controversial groups. Don't write checks for any incriminating or politically incorrect pleasures. Withdraw the money, take it to the post office or Western Union and purchase a money order. These money orders are anonymous until you write your name on them, and no one but you and the recipient

---

[1] Be careful, though. The IRS has begun checking these places for possible use by those nasty old tax resisters. You can avoid some of the risk by using several services, perhaps in different towns, adopting two or more identities (documents required), and discreetly questioning the business about its policies and its contacts with the government. Do what I would do; call, tell them you're a writer researching a book on privacy, and ask your questions.

have a record. Banks sell money orders, too, but theirs are usually more expensive, and they generally ask for the recipient's name and keep both your name and the recipient's in their records.

- Consider opening a foreign savings account and getting an offshore debit card. (See *Cover your assets,* No. 35.)

Once people think you're bad, you might as well be bad. It's more fun than being good.
    — Sue Grafton, writer

69. Create a fake plot or organization

In one city that shall remain nameless, local libertarians have created the Real People's Liberation Front (RPLF, melodiously pronounced "Ripple-fuh"). Ripple-fuh's "leader," Subcommandante Patrick Henry, and his lieutenant, Dagny Taggart, issue communiqués declaring April 15 to be April Fools' Day and coronate their friends King of the County (on the theory that local government isn't representative anyway, so why pretend?).

After a period of ignoring the group's initial news releases, the press got into the spirit and began printing the subcommandante's pronouncements. One newspaper even arranged a "secret" interview with "Patrick Henry," complete with face-masked photo of the Glorious Leader.

Ripple-fuh is all in good fun — a palatable way of poking fun at bureaucratic pomposity and bringing government down to its proper level.

All it takes to create a group like this is one person, a word processor, a fax machine, a little flair for PR, and a sense of humor. No harm to anything except a few politicians' egos.

If you want it, here's a nice name for your group, courtesy of my friend, Charles Curley: The Society for Creative Anarchism. Have fun.

But seriously...

You could use the same tools to create a much more serious fake organization — a "clandestine, underground" group that gives the impression of real menace. If you go this route, *never* do more than create an impression. Don't threaten anybody, don't plant even fake explosives, don't actually *be* menacing in any way, shape or form. The penalties would absolutely not be worth it, if you got caught. Anyway, the object here is not to foment a revolution or stir hate; it's merely to send paranoid officials on a wild goose chase and watch the media make a fool of itself.

To accomplish this, you can send mysterious messages to officials (thinly coded, easily decipherable, but ultimately saying nothing that makes sense), tag buildings with symbols of your "group," issue manifestos, claim growing membership, send letters to the editor or news releases bragging of non-existent accomplishments, spread vague rumors about the doings of some powerful new group (like mass paramilitary training exercises in the woods just outside of town), and otherwise scare the pants off the already paranoid powers-that-be.

In the rumor department, get a few trusted friends to help you. Make sure the rumor is always something the person "knows" is true because his next door neighbor's cousin had a friend who was *there*.

If government and media people are ready to imagine "right-wing terrorists" under every rock, give them evidence to prove it. Then sit back and enjoy their foolishness.

Whether humorous or scary, it's easiest if your "group" operates locally, not nationally. However, if you create a really scary one, you might get national attention. Then, provided you haven't done anything illegal, you can get a big laugh by letting the hysteria build, then revealing the whole thing was a hoax, kind of like those two guys did in Britain a few years back when they announced they'd created those "mysterious, supernatural" crop circles all by themselves, as a joke.

There's also the potential fun of having three friends in three cities with three fax machines joining in...or five or ten... provided you measure the risk of one of them blowing your cover before you're ready.

Note: To keep faxes from pointing right at you, you must either zap them from public fax places or, better, remove or falsify the identifying number your machine automatically sends. You can do that easily by typing in a new setting. The manual that came with your fax tells how. Doesn't it just figure, removing this number is a federal crime — so of course no one is recommending that you do it. But among the eleven million pages of federal crimes, this one is right up there in order of seriousness with failing to answer the census. Oh, they could get you for it; that's what most federal law is for — not curtailing evildoers, but giving feds a hook to control you and me. However, if that's all you're guilty of, they'd look pretty silly prosecuting you.

A regulation can be for a fool to obey and a wise man to break.
—Sir Hugh Trenchard, Founder of the Royal Air Force

70. Create a real organization

If it takes only one person and a fax machine to create a fake organization, how many people do you think it takes to create a real one?

How many left-wing organizations, widely quoted and taken extremely seriously by the media, are not much more than one or two people with a good sense of PR and the sympathies of the press?

It's harder to be taken seriously if you are libertarian or right-wing, but not impossible if you are persistent and professional in your approach, or if you live in an area small enough for the media to be desperate for stories. Here are some tips:

- Choose a good, memorable, believable name.
- Design a professional-looking letterhead. Anybody can do it these days with a simple desktop publishing program. Print letterhead, envelopes and business cards on decent quality stock.
- If possible, get a few prominent people to agree to be on your "board of directors," then print their names in a column on the side of the stationery. This precise fraud is committed by virtually every charitable or political organization in the country. You don't really think those lists of VIPs actually participate in the organizations, do you? No, they're just prostituting their names.
- Pick a cause and stick to it. Don't get side-tracked. This is the way to create an identity for the media. Remember, they're lazy and not always that bright, so you need to make yourself stand out in their minds. Then, when they've got to do a story on X they'll say, "Oh, I'll just call Jo Blow for a quote."
- Send frequent, brief news releases, either announcing news of your own or commenting on current issues

pertinent to your cause. Strive for a professional tone; never rant; use facts and good quotes when possible. Never send a news release unless you have something the media could construe as real news or factual information. They'll tune them out if you bombard them with nothing but fluff and opinion.

- Be your own spokesperson, or enlist an articulate friend.
- Avoid damning the media. You need them, even when you hate them. But do feel free to request retractions if they get facts wrong, and lobby to be allowed to present guest editorials on your group's behalf.
- If possible, offer yourself or a member as an on-call expert on whatever issue you're focusing on. It's best if you actually are an expert, but as long as you can make a statement sound good, expertise doesn't always matter.
- Avoid answering questions about the size of your membership. When necessary, lie. But you'd be surprised how often such questions *don't* come up.

71. Join the tax protesters on April 15

I'm not talking about tax resistance, here. That's a different subject. I'm talking about showing up at your local post office on the late afternoon and evening of tax day to greet the late filers and get some media attention.

Many local Libertarian Party chapters have been doing this for years. You can join them or put together your own protest.

The important thing is to have fun and let the weary taxpayers know you're on their side. Don't take yourself too seriously. Don't make the people feel worse than they already do. Don't use it as an opportunity to present heavy philosophical issues. Just be there, presenting your message in a colorful, lovable way. You'll gain brownie points for it and be remembered fondly.

Some surefire ideas:

- Wave "Honk if You Hate Taxes" signs.
- Have someone dress up as the president and thank people for their generous contributions as they drive up to the boxes. President and first lady masks should be available at any costume rental store.
- Hand out "million-dollar bills." These are available from the national Libertarian Party (address given in *If you must vote (part I)*....No. 90). They remind people the federal government spends that much money every five minutes.
- Have someone dress up as Paul Revere or Patrick Henry.
- Have a young lady dress down as Lady Godiva (whose famous ride was a tax protest). Put her on a real or fake horse, wearing a bikini or flesh-colored body stocking.

You'll need to check local regulations before you go out. Your city might require a permit for a demonstration. You can hand out literature, but never force it on anyone or impede the flow of traffic to the mailboxes.

Be sure to let the post office know you're coming. This is, first of all, a courtesy. But it might also give you a chance to prevent officials from causing problems. They frequently tell protesters they're forbidden to petition on government property. It's nonsense, but you may need to show them a copy of the law, or even get your state attorney general to intercede before they'll back down. That takes time.

And don't forget to notify the media! Even when they don't like your political position, they lo-o-o-o-ve this kind of colorful event.

America was neither founded, nor freed, by the well behaved.
— An audience member on a Seattle TV talk show, discussing drug legalization

72. Learn Dumpster diving
What a disgusting idea, crawling around in other people's garbage in search of food and other useable (or salable) goodies, but what a useful skill if you want to live cheaply... if the country goes into depression... if you're on the run with no money... if the government's taken everything you own.

Hey, you can even use it to curry favor with your environmentalist friends. After all, you're making the ultimate personal commitment to recycling!

To learn the best tools and techniques, times and places, and even how to handle run-ins with the Dumpster police, check out *The Art and Science of Dumpster Diving* by John Hoffman (Loompanics Unlimited, 1993).

73. Get healthy!
"Oh God," you groan. "Every health fascist in the universe rags on me to eat my vegetables, lighten up on the Big Macs and stomp on a stair-stepper. Now I'm even getting that lecture in a book about preparing for revolution."

Yes. You are.

74. Learn to disappear in a crowd
Here's something fun to try that could also save your life. Practice invisibility. That is, practice being in various kinds of crowds and public settings and blending in so perfectly that no one really sees you.

Try being the perfect fan at a football game, even if you detest the sport. Try being the tweedy professor on a college campus, even if you didn't make it past high school. Be the tired mother at the grocery store, the sharp reporter at the crime scene, the business executive at the airport, the street person in the plaza.

Pick somebody, pick a *type* of somebody. Then *become* them.

This is not so much a matter of disguise as a matter of grooming, walk, facial expression, dress, objects you carry, tone of voice, word choice and so on. You'll also find, as you observe, that it's a matter of learning to think and feel like the people you're imitating.

This valuable skill could help you "hide in plain sight" someday, to perform an act of freedom fighting or hide from police. In addition to that, though, you'll discover that your increased powers of observation will help you understand people better and predict their actions and reactions. That could help you if you ever had to persuade or deceive someone to save your life.

If you are especially tall or fat, if you have distinctive coloring, gorgeous hair, a funny goatee, a bad scar or something else that, by itself, makes you stand out in a crowd, this is more of a challenge, of course. But even if you're not a candidate for really "disappearing," it's still a good skill to learn and a fun game to play.

There are some books on this one, too. Try: *Disguise Techniques: Fool All of the People Some of the Time*, by Edmond A. MacInaugh, or for one that focuses more heavily on disguise than on acting: *Methods of Disguise*, by John Sample. The latter is available from Loompanics.

Men who borrow their opinions can never repay their debts.
　　— George Savile, Marquis of Halifax

75. Find a balance point in dealing with people

To live among your fellow humans, it helps to understand what they feel and how they think. This requires sensitive antennae and years of trial and error, but that sensitivity enables us to get along with our neighbors, co-workers and family members without constantly tromping on their feelings and creating chaos.

Unfortunately, the very sensitivity that is a valuable survival skill also gets in the way of our independent thinking and action. We're reluctant to advocate drug legalization or anarchism because we don't want people to dismiss us as wingnuts. We give our Social Security number because we don't want to get "that look" from a clerk or bureaucrat. We keep our mouths shut in the face of injustice because we don't want a reputation as a troublemaker. We "go along to get along" in the workplace because we don't want someone saying, "He's not a team player."

We need to find a balance between caring what other people feel and preserving our own feelings, thoughts, rights and lives. It's easy in theory, but a bitch in practice.

Spend some time considering when it's better to give in for the sake of living with others and when it's better to take a stand to live with yourself.

So it was "freedom" as defined by Orwell and Kafka, "freedom" as granted by Stalin and Hitler, the "freedom" to pace back and forth in your cage.
　　— Robert A. Heinlein, *The Cat Who Walks Through Walls*

76. Follow your bliss

You hold back from doing what you really want because the ghost voices of parents and past teachers nag in your head, "It's foolish, boy," "It's impractical, girl."

You "know" you couldn't make a living as an artist, hitchhike around the world, build a better mousetrap, live off the land, build a cabin in the woods, invent cold fusion, write the Great American Novel, raise sheep for a living, move to a mountaintop, be self-employed, live in a hamlet in Vermont, join a monastery, lead an insurgency movement or build wooden clocks for a living.

But you only "know" because other people told you so.

Whose life is it, anyway? Does it belong to you, or to the ghost of your third-grade teacher?

What's the worst that can happen to you if you follow your inner voice on what someone else believes is an impractical course? You could die? So what? You're going to die anyway. You could fail, be laughed at and have to listen to "I told you so"?

Well, I agree that's worse than dying, but the proper answer is a steady gaze right in the eye and a firm, proud, "At least *I* tried."

More important, what's the best thing that can happen? Freedom? Fun? Wealth? Happiness? Fame? Satisfaction? A sense of contentment at the end of the day?

Isn't it worth going for?

Now, having said that, prepare yourself as best you can before you take the leap. Do your best to make sure you've built the necessary skills, have the needed resources, and are going at it with the right attitude.

Follow your bliss — but don't leave your brain behind.

"But look," said Ponder, "The graveyards are full of people who rushed in bravely but unwisely."

"Ook." [said the orangutan]

"What'd he say?" said the Bursar...

"I think he said, 'Sooner or later the graveyards are full of everybody,'" said Ponder. "Oh blast. Come on."
— Terry Pratchett, *Lords & Ladies*

A special section on preparedness
In the aftermath of the latest Florida hurricane, the media blitzed us with images of desperate parents who didn't even have milk or uncontaminated water to give their babies.

This was supposed to reduce us to paroxysms of pity.

A more responsible reaction was: What kind of criminally uncaring mother or father would deliberately put a baby at such risk?

These hurricane survivors weren't victims whose homes and possessions had been destroyed. They were simply people who didn't bother to keep a few days supply of life's necessities around the house. They knew they lived at risk of hurricanes. They knew Andrew was coming. They knew their children had to have food and water, but they figured someone else would take care of them.

Something as simple as a few days interruption in the normal supply line left their children's lives in danger.

You wouldn't be so foolish, would you?

Every adult should be prepared to take care of him or herself through a time of crisis. Every parent should be prepared to take care of children.

Yours could be a short-term crisis, like a flood or hurricane, or a long-term crisis, such as a war, depression, sustained unemployment, major illness or social collapse. *If you claim to believe in independence, it's up to you to be as prepared as possible to survive whatever nature, life and the government throw at you.*

Naturally, it's daunting. Unless you're wealthy and/or obsessed, it's nearly impossible to lay in all possible supplies you might need to sustain you through hardship, let alone develop every possible survival skill. Even if all you do is put $5.00 per week and a few hours thought toward emergency food and keep a few how-to books on your shelves, you're better off than if you do nothing at all.

A preparedness plan has many parts. For purposes of this book, I've broken the basic plan into eight major areas, with a few extras to follow. The basics are:

- Your grab & go kit
- Water
- Food
- Medical/health
- Weapons
- Other equipment
- Resources
- Skills

77. Your three-day grab & go kit

The Red Cross says that, in event of disaster, you should be prepared to care for yourself and your family for three full days. That's how long it takes, on average, before emergency personnel and supplies are readily available. Keep in mind that *is* an average. You could face an even longer wait.

You might also have to hit the road in a hurry for a variety of other reasons. In that case, your three-day kit could sustain you until you reached your hidden stash or a place of safety.

Keep in a duffel bag or backpack, either in a vehicle or near a door of your house:

- Enough food for 72 hours. This should be something that requires no cooking or preparation. Granola bars or high-energy food bars will do. Military MREs (meals-ready-to-eat) are better, though a lot more expensive.
- A 72-hour water supply. For a grab-and-go kit, you can buy foil packets of water from survival goods stores, which are very portable, though rather expensive.
- Lightweight blankets. (Survival stores carry mylar "space blankets," which can be helpful in some circumstances— like when you need to be visible to searchers — but they aren't a good substitute for woven blankets.)
- Toilet paper.
- Waterproof matches (or other firestarters), candles and/or a lantern.
- A first-aid kit.
- Other items you can't live without.

You should have a kit for each member of your family. Keep it handy, and if you're forced to run from your house, it might keep you alive until help comes.

78. Building your emergency water supply

The next part of your preparedness plan is easy, cheap, and takes almost no effort. All you need to do is set aside enough water to take care of your drinking and sanitation needs during any emergency in which you might remain at home.

The minimum supply is three days. A better supply is ten. Better yet, a month. If you're planning to endure a state of siege or a major ecological disaster, you might want to prepare for several months.

For basic preparedness, here's all you have to do:

- Figure one gallon per person per day for drinking and hygiene, two gallons if you plan to be cooking with water or re-hydrating dried foods.
- Start saving one-gallon milk jugs. As you empty each one, wash it thoroughly, fill it with clean tap water, add a single drop of bleach (Unscented, please! Some additives can kill you.), write the date on the jug, and put it away. In a few weeks, you'll have a basic supply for your family.
- If you haven't used the water within a year, empty each jug and fill it with fresh.

You can also buy plastic 55-gallon water drums or five-gallon plastic containers, build an underground tank, or use the water from your waterbed (depending on whether or not you've put toxic chemicals in it). If your area has sufficient rain water, you can catch runoff from your roof in a barrel. Keep a lid on the barrel, and funnel water in through a downspout. In any case, be sure to add a little bleach to the supply.

Warning: Keep a supply of water on hand even if you have a plentiful natural water supply nearby. An earthquake could shut off the flow from your spring. An electrical outage could leave you unable to pump from your well. After a flood, forest fire, bombing, storm or ecological catastrophe, contamination — from rotting bodies to landfill wastes to radiation — could make water from rivers and lakes undrinkable. (In fact, most already is undrinkable, due to *giardia* and other pollutants.)

If you plan to use such a supply, you should purchase a water filtration system from one of the suppliers listed in *Some places to find all of the above,* No. 83. These are usually expensive and rely on replaceable filters that can run out just when you need them. But they beat dying of some water-borne bug. You can also purchase various water purification tablets or simply boil all drinking water.

The man who produces while others dispose of his product is a slave.
— Ayn Rand

79. Building your emergency food supply

Without a doubt, food is the most expensive part of this proposition, especially if you have a family. But if you start slowly, and build steadily you can do it. It might help to gradually build a food plan around three lines of defense:

- The one-month basic supply
- The three- to six-month backup supply
- The long-term survival supply

You can build these up in stages, buying what you can afford at the time.

The one-month basic supply

This one's pretty easy because it consists of the ordinary canned and packaged foods you eat every day. You can build this supply simply by adding a few extra items to your weekly grocery list.

The basic component of your 30-day supply should be items that last a long time with no special storage methods, require little preparation and may, if necessary, be eaten straight out of the can or box. Next, you want items that can be quickly prepared by adding water or a few other basic ingredients. In that case, your supply might look something like this:

- Canned beans

- Canned chili
- Canned fruits
- Canned vegetables
- Packaged dry soups
- Boxed macaroni and cheese
- Boxed instant potatoes
- Non-fat dry milk
- Margarine or butter (if you have a means of keeping them cool; if not, powdered versions of these are available from survival stores)
- Pancake mix
- Dried fruit
- Salt, pepper and other spices you commonly use
- Spaghetti noodles
- Jars of prepared spaghetti sauce
- Egg noodles
- Canned tuna
- Canned chicken
- Crackers
- Cereals
- Nuts
- Chips and other snack foods
- Honey or sugar

Always buy foods you regularly eat, and keep them rotating with your everyday items. Canned foods do not make good long-term storage items, since they are good only for a year or two (at most).

To the above list, add any of your own favorites and delete anything you don't like. To satisfy fresh food cravings, you can also add long-lasting fresh fruits and vegetables to this list — provided they are items you regularly eat and can keep a rotating supply of. In that case, consider apples, oranges, grapefruit, carrots and potatoes.

If you have your own veggie garden, bee hives, goats, cattle or chickens, all the better. If you're equipped for preserving your own foods in a root cellar, by dehydration, or canning, you're really in great shape for a month or much, much more.

The three- to six-month backup supply

This is where you begin bringing in specially prepared and packed "survival foods," available by mail order from the stores listed below. These foods are dehydrated or freeze-dried, and packed in #10 or #2½ cans for long-term storage.

They will last anywhere from five years to forever, depending on the item. (Powdered milk or butter, for instance, will have a relatively short life; grains and pasta are far more durable. Manufacturers provide charts showing shelf-lives, but these can't always be believed. I suggest you compare shelf-lives of several brands and use the most conservative figures as your guide.)

The foods packaged this way range from things that require a lot of preparation and mixing with other ingredients (like cheese powder, dried mushrooms or powdered margarine), to items you can munch right out of the can (like dried apples or pilot bread), to fancy, pre-prepared dinners (like the yummy Leonardo da Fettucini and vegetarian Mountain Chili sold by Alpine Aire).

You can buy these items by the can, by the case, or in a variety of kits designed for long-term use (one-month basic supply, three-month basic supply, one-year basic supply, one-year deluxe supply, six month supply with meat, etc.).

Most kits aren't a good buy. They tend to contain items that won't fit into your personal eating habits. The affordable ones contain things that aren't always even identifiable. (Someday, I intend to ask one of these marketers just what the heck "fruit galaxy" is; whatever it may be, it's in every budget-priced survival food supply on the planet.) The affordable ones might also lull you into a false sense of security; some "year's supplies" would give you only about 900 calories a day over that period, slowly starving you to death.

The really great kits, with 2,000+ calories a day and a variety of delicious items, tend to run to mega bucks. Better to build your own supply over time.

In addition to these packaged foods, you can also lay in a supply of military MREs. Created for the U.S. armed forces, and packed in handy pouches, these are available either as entrees or as full meals. They're not bad. Except for a slight metallic taste, some are delicious. They're a bit on the expensive side (perhaps $1.20+ for an entree and $3.00+ for a meal, as of this writing), but you might store some to use as a treat or when you don't feel like preparing your dried foods.

Your home canned and stored items can also help you get through a few months of deprivation. Just remember, though, they lose their nutritional value after a year or two and are not suitable for long-term storage.

The long-term survival supply

A true long-term supply will contain a little of all of the above. You definitely want variety, not monotony. If you're facing a long period of economic hardship — like that caused by a sustained illness, unemployment or nationwide depression — you'll want to add a final layer of very fundamental, durable foods to your storage plan.

These items are nitrogen-packed in five- or six-gallon buckets for very long storage. They include such very basic basics as:

- Wheat (hard red winter wheat is best)
- Beans
- Oatmeal
- Split peas
- Corn kernels
- Barley
- Honey
- Lentils
- And other durable, unprocessed items

Some of these require special equipment to prepare. Wheat, for instance, isn't much use without a grinder to produce flour or cracked grain cereal, but buckets of staples are reasonably priced. A 45-pounder can run as little as $18, depending on the item. The most expensive, honey, might run you $60 a bucket.

Though I consider these for long-term storage, they can also make a cheap addition to your everyday food supply. For instance, if you eat a lot of oatmeal, make tons of pea soup, or love homemade bread from the freshest whole-wheat flour, these big buckets could be just the thing.

80. Building your medical kit

At an absolute minimum you need:

- A first-aid kit large and varied enough to meet the needs of your household. You might need to add extras, depending on your particular risks — e.g., a snakebite kit, blankets for treating hypothermia, etc.
- A good supply of any medications you require to stay alive and functioning. A year's worth is best. You should

keep this stash in a cool, dark, dry place and rotate in new supplies, since drugs deteriorate over time.

- Backup medications such as antibiotics, anti-diarrhea and anti-nausea medicines, pain killers and others you might need while cut off from your regular medical suppliers.

- Some good books on diagnosis and treatment. Try to include a Red Cross first aid book, the *Merck Manual* and the *Physicians' Desk Reference.* If you are into alternative medicine or might need to doctor yourself without "civilized" medical supplies, try Bradford Angier's *How to Be Your Own Wilderness Doctor* and similar titles.

> *This country was founded by religious nuts with guns.*
> — P.J. O'Rourke

81. Your survival-weapons supply

In a short-term emergency, you might need firearms to protect yourself, family, home or business. Who can forget the footage of Korean shopkeepers in Los Angeles saving their businesses from the depredations of rioters after the first Rodney King verdict?

In a long-term emergency, you may need to hunt to survive, and you may still need to defend your home against gangs of marauders better prepared and better armed than the L.A. rioters.

When it comes to recommending firearms and other weapons, you can be sure of only one thing: gun people are opinionated. Any firearms devotee is bound to disagree with at least one of the suggested weapons on my list. Some will disagree with the entire list. A few will not only disagree with the entire list, but insist I'm a complete idiot, from a long line of complete idiots who shouldn't be allowed out in public without a label on my forehead warning that I could be hazardous to your health.

There are thousands of weapons to choose from. There are millions of individual tastes and lifestyles, and the very subject of guns provokes a kind of religious fervor among some people, causing them to believe their choices are the *only* possible choices.

With that in mind, I will tell you that the following list is nothing more than my personal opinion, based on my research and what I perceive to be a typical need. It is a place for you to begin if you haven't already studied the subject on your own. It is, furthermore, the list of a person who:

- Recommends mid-priced weapons over both cheap junk and "Mercedes" guns;
- Thinks that, for most purposes, weapons should come out of the box ready for use without expensive customization;
- Does not hunt for pleasure;
- And considers guns to be useful tools, not a hobby or a religion.

You should, of course, never buy any weapon solely on anyone else's recommendation. Think about your own needs, then examine a variety of weapons that might be suitable. Rent some handguns from your local shooting range or borrow handguns, rifles and shotguns from friendly gun owners. Try them out. See how they feel, and how you feel about them. (Before you do anything else, learn safe handling techniques, please!)

Now, having said that, here's my idea of a decent survival weapons supply. If I had a very limited budget, I'd begin with the following:

1. A short-barreled, pump-action or semi-automatic, full cylinder bore shotgun for home defense. The Mossberg

Model 500, Winchester Defender and Remington 870 are the classics. A weapon like this can spread shot over a wide area, saving you from having to aim perfectly in the dark or in panic conditions. But unlike a bullet from a pistol or rifle, shot isn't likely to go through a wall and kill a neighbor or other innocent bystander.

2. A multi-purpose rifle to protect against both four-legged and two-legged varmints at greater ranges. My choice would be the Ruger Mini-14 in .223 cal, or the Ruger Mini-30 in 7.62 x 39 mm. On a budget, I'd go for a Chinese or Russian SKS in 7.62 x 39, but these aren't as well made and don't have the range of the Rugers. Though it's illegal in many places, you could also take deer with these calibers if you had to.

3. A handgun for self-defense. I'd choose a .45 semi-automatic like the classic Colt 1911 (now copied by dozens of manufacturers) or the Glock 21. You'll have to have fairly large hands to grip the latter, but it's a reliable, easy-to-use weapon that can take all kinds of abuse. Other semi-auto calibers I'd consider: 10mm, .40 Smith & Wesson and 9mm. If you like revolvers, look at .357 magnum or .45 long Colt. Nothing smaller, please! Don't go out and get a .25 or a .32 because you're inexperienced, have small hands or are afraid of big guns. Instead, get some experience, overcome your fears, or find a large caliber gun with a grip that fits smaller hands. A gun that is too underpowered may not have the stopping power you need to save your life in an emergency.

4. Basic survival rifle/shotgun combination. This usually means a gun that can shoot either a single .22 long rifle round or a .410 shot shell. It can be useful if you need game, any game, and don't know what you might run into while you're on the prowl.

Then, as I acquired more money, I'd add the following to my arsenal:

1. A bolt action rifle for hunting deer, elk and other large game. Many calibers are available, but .308, 30-06, .270 and 7 mm are among the popular ones, depending on the game you're after, the distances you need to cover, and your personal preferences. A *good* bolt action rifle (not a $200 '98 Mauser!) with a very high-quality scope is what you need if you intend to take up sniping.

2. A long-barreled shotgun for hunting wildfowl. Again, there are infinite choices and I have no particular preference.

3. A handgun for serious game shooting and defense against wild animals. This means either a .44 magnum or a .41 magnum revolver. Either of these will kill a grizzly bear if you had to, in self-defense. Nobody recommends you go bear hunting with this weapon. It can also be used to take deer and other sizable game at ranges up to 100 yards (if you're a good shot and have a scope).

4. An air rifle for killing tiny varmints (rats and bats) and hunting small game like squirrels. Ideally, this should be a high-quality European variety, not a $60 Daisy. I pant for a Feinwerkbau 124, which is old, but incredibly accurate and reliable. Many other German air guns have come on the market since I first fell in love with the FWB.

5. A slingshot. You can buy one for $5.00 at any sporting goods store. You'll need to practice your buns off to be any good at it. But in a pinch, it may be all you have.

6. A crossbow. Again, a weapon for when you've lost everything else or for when you need to commit serious damage in serious silence. A crossbow bolt can go straight through a tree, but since it doesn't expand (as bullets do), you have to be a pretty accurate shot to

defend yourself or kill an animal. One great advantage: it's quiet enough to kill, for instance, a concentration camp guard or other goon, without anyone knowing right away.

You'll also need plenty of ammo for all of the above, of course. An adequate supply might be 1000 rounds for a semi-automatic rifle, 1000 pellets for an air gun, 500 rounds each for pistols and bolt-action rifles, a like number of steel balls for your slingshot, 100-250 shotgun shells, and perhaps 100 crossbow bolts. This sounds like a lot, but you'll find you can use up hundreds of rounds a day just in practice.

(You are going to practice, aren't you? And having practiced, you're going to re-stock your ammo supply, right?)

The particular *types* of ammunition are very important. For instance, for your handgun, you'll want inexpensive round-nose (ball) ammo for practice, but a good hollow point (like Federal Hydra-Shok) or specialty ammo (like Glaser Safety Slugs or MagSafe) for self defense. These rounds are designed to spread when they hit, doing maximum damage to your target, yet being less likely to go straight through and hit someone standing behind him.

Ammo is much too complex to go into here. If you don't know what's best for your purpose, ask the people at your local gun store. They'll know — and will talk your ear off.

Bow hunters will say I've neglected their weapon, and I have. I don't know enough about bow and arrow to assess their use in survival situations. They certainly have the advantage of silence. If that method appeals to you, you can find bow hunters' magazines in most grocery stores or track down a friend who enjoys the hobby and look into it.

If the above list was all Greek to you, talk with the people at a sizable gun store or sporting goods store. They'll help. Members of a local gun club will also be pleased to offer advice. In fact, once you start talking with gunnies, advice is the one thing you'll always have an abundance of.

82. Start thinking about tools & equipment

Tools and equipment: This nice, vague category could go on for chapters. So I'll just offer some basics, then refer you to survival catalogs for more. Also see *Read: self reliance*, No. 48, for other survival tools and tactics.

If you are planning for the long term, think about getting:

- A grinder for grains and nuts. Electric models are available, but then you'll need a steady power supply, either your own or your community's. A tiny, but very useable hand grinder can be had for around $55, but the price quickly jumps to $300 or so for nice stone-grinders.
- Veggie seeds. Buy them sealed in a can, specially selected for survival needs. If you buy at your local garden supply store, you must be very careful not to choose hybrid varieties since you will not be able to collect and use their seed for future crops. (Hybrids don't reproduce true, and may not reproduce at all.)
- An alternative cooking method. If your power is out for days, weeks or months, you'll need another way of warming food. There are plenty, and you may already have one in your camping supplies. These include white gas stoves, propane stoves, butane stoves, solar cookers, charcoal cookers and wood-burning. You can use your regular electric stove, if you power it with a solar system. Choose one or two that best suit your needs. Be careful; some — like charcoal burners — should never be used indoors, thanks to their output of carbon monoxide.
- An alternate light source. A Coleman gas lantern or butane lamp will do, provided you make sure to have plenty of fuel and extra mantels on hand.

- An alternate heat source for your home. Kerosene will do in the short term. A wood burner is better in the long run, provided you have a reliable supply of fuel. Solar is the very best, as long as your climate is suitable and your budget can stand it.

- A method of power generation. One of those little gas Honda generators is okay in an emergency. But if you're really serious about surviving off-grid (or when the grid has been switched off) consider a good solar system, wind generator (depending, again, on your climate) or a China diesel generator. There are a lot of other methods, from water-driven ram pumps to pedal power. *Backwoods Home* magazine, listed in *Read: self-reliance,* No. 48, is a good source for a lot more information on this topic.

- A method of sanitation. If "civilized" services are cut off, you might not have the use of your toilet. In the long term, then, you'll want to build an outhouse or have a composting toilet. Chemical toilets of the type used in boats and RVs can be useful. In a dire, but short-term emergency try this: cut a hole in the top of a wooden box or sturdy cardboard box. Anchor a plastic garbage bag inside. (You can tape it to the sides of a cardboard box, or staple it to wood.) Use it. Add some outhouse lime (available from farm supply stores) and cover for odor control. Dispose of the bag after a couple of days.

83. Some places to find all of the above

You can purchase emergency food and other survival supplies from the companies listed on the next pages. There are many other sources, but these are the ones I personally know to be reliable suppliers of quality stuff:

The Survival Center
P.O. Box 234
McKenna, Washington 98558
voice: (360) 458-6778
fax: (360) 458-6868
order line: 1-800-321-2900
e-mail: sales@survivalcenter.com
Web site: http://www.survivalcenter.com
   The Survival Center has a large supply of nearly everything
— food, tools and hundreds of books. Prices are fair (though
not spectacular) and service is excellent. Send $2.00 for a
catalog.

Emergency Essentials
353 N. State Street
Orem, Utah 84057
voice: (801) 222-9596
fax: (801) 222-9598
order line: 1-800-999-1863
e-mail: catalogsales@beprepared.com
Web site: http://www.beprepared.com
   This company also has a large supply, including tents,
backpacks, water filtration systems, foul weather equipment,
as well as a large selection of food items. Prices are fair, and
their periodic catalogs often have good sales. I've personally
found their customer service to be mediocre. On one
occasion they told me five different times that an item would
be shipped "in a week," and they seemed not to give a damn
what I thought of the situation, but they do ultimately deliver
what they promise.

Future Foods
1448 West 1250 South
Orem, Utah 84058
voice: (801) 224-3663

fax: (801) 221-0336
1-800-949-FOOD (3663)
This company specializes in emergency food supplies only. These are basic items, nothing fancy. Future Foods' prices are the best (particularly if you sign up as a member) and their service is adequate and friendly. They'll send a free catalog on request.

Alpine Aire
P.O. Box 926
Nevada City, California 95959
voice: (916) 272-1971
order line: 1-800-322-6325
fax: (916) 272-2624
e-mail: alpineaire@mtmarketplace.com
Web site: http://www.alpineaire.com

If you're looking for the best quality in both food and service, Alpine Aire is your place. All of the suppliers mentioned here carry good quality storage foods, but Alpine Aire also sells "gourmet" prepared dinners and specialty items (like sour cream powder and dried strawberries) that are almost impossible to find elsewhere. Their foods are all natural and contain no preservatives, coloring agents, white sugar or MSG. In addition to their line of #10 and #2½ canned goods, they also market dinners in foil packets, suitable for elegant backpacking excursions. Their full-color catalog is free for the asking.

Also check out:

- Your local Red Cross office for publications and videos on emergency procedures
- Local outdoor and camping stores
- Hardware stores

84. Building your skills

It takes more than "things" to make a good survival plan. Consider developing one or more of these skills. Some can help you survive an immediate crisis; others could be handy in a long-term economic crunch, when you must barter your skills for goods and services.

- Gunsmithing
- Welding
- Carpentry
- Food-canning and other storage
- Small-appliance repair
- Computer repair
- Gardening
- Care of dairy and meat animals
- First aid and CPR
- More advanced home doctoring
- Home chiropractic care
- Teaching of basic skills (reading, writing, 'rithmatic)
- Sewing
- Quilting
- Cooking with storage foods
- Auto and other machinery repair
- Pottery making
- Well-digging and/or water-witching
- Herb gardening and herbal medicines
- Horseback riding
- Bicycle repair
- Fishing
- Hunting
- Orienteering (for survival in the wilderness)
- Recognizing edible (and poisonous!) wild plants
- Recognizing wild plants with medicinal value

* Public speaking

I'm sure you can think of many, many more.
Liberty means responsibility. That is why most men dread it.

— George Bernard Shaw

It's difficult enough to prepare for our own well-being. The next section covers even tougher subjects: preparing our children, our pets and our aging relatives for hard times. This section is brief. You could write whole books about this. So I simply offer some tips to get you started thinking about your own family's needs.

85. Prepare your children, pets and aging relatives

First, the kids

Preparing your children to survive hard times depends a lot on how old they are, what your circumstances are, and what type of troubles you anticipate. A few things to consider:

* Some children will die before eating unfamiliar or unpleasant foods. Keep a good supply of familiar staples on hand. If you plan to stock canned survival foods, be sure to begin integrating them into your family's diet long before you need them. Unless you live in a rural area, your only milk supply in a crisis might be powdered non-fat milk. Make sure your kids are used to it, so they don't reject "that yukky blue stuff" when they have nothing else to drink. Stock a good supply of treats, as well, preferably healthy ones.

* Make sure you have at least a year's supply of any regular medication your children require. Store it in a cool, dry, dark place and rotate new supplies in regularly, since drugs deteriorate over time. (*The Physicians' Desk Reference*, available at your library reference desk — and

perhaps part of your medical kit — will give you information about shelf-lives.)

- If you're a believer in preparedness, you probably already have a first-aid kit and at least a few medicines on hand. For children, you might require a few extras. Consider: a larger supply of bandages and ointments for cuts, scrapes & sprains; a vaporizer, salves and liquids to treat colds, children's pain reliever, several kinds of antibiotics effective for different conditions, anti-nausea and anti-diarrhea medicines, extra splints for small broken limbs and a big supply of calamine lotion for skin rashes. If you explain to your doctor that you're putting together an emergency kit, he or she might be willing to prescribe the medicines you require.

- Kids can be astoundingly materialistic. If you buy yours every toy advertised on TV, you could be setting yourself up for a struggle in tough times. It's hard for kids to understand "We can't afford that," when they see you "affording" food, rent, clothes and gas for your car. Just as you need to prepare yourself *now* to do without later, you especially need to prepare your children. Cut down on the number and lavishness of "bought" toys. Start making handmade toys, playing inexpensive card games or word games, and improvising family games of your own. Encourage kids to draw, write, or develop a simple hobby like wildflower collecting. Let them make their own toys. Teach them strategic games like chess (which will help them think for themselves). You'll find that all this not only costs less, but helps you pull together as a family when the time comes.

- Teach your children about the Constitution and Bill of Rights, or about other political values you hold dear. They'll be better prepared to understand, when the bad times come, that the government — not you or blind fate — caused the problem. Let them know that even children can stand up and defend their rights.

- Teach them to keep family activities confidential. This flies in the face of what they're taught in school and by the media, which is to tell all. In fact, there's wisdom on both sides. No child should have to suffer abuse in the name of keeping "family business" private. On the other hand, your children should learn when silence is wisdom — when silence might save their lives or keep their parents out of jail. (It's a tough one, that.)
- Be prepared to teach them at home. Have lots of books on hand, in a variety of subjects, and geared to several levels of ability. There's no telling how long you might be on your own in educating your kids. Also learn to recognize the opportunities for learning that exist in nature, in your community, and in everyday activities.
- Have a plan for coping if you must hit the road. Will you take your children with you or leave them with a relative? If you take them, plan a kit including toys, special foods, extra clothes, medicines, etc. Be prepared for dealing with their impatience on long road trips or during periods when you might be cooped up in isolated places.

Then Fido and Fluffy

I hate to say it, but the first thing you have to ask yourself is: Could I eat Fido if things really got bad?

My personal answer to that question is no. I'd die before I'd eat a pet. Your answer might be different. The main thing is to *know*. You also need to ask yourself whether you could kill Fido if you couldn't feed him any more, or if you needed to run and couldn't take him with you.

Assuming you prefer Fido, Fluffy or Mike the Iguana alive, well and at your side, here are some things to do:

- Lay in a several month supply of your pet's food. A year's worth is better. If it's bulk food, not canned, you'll need to store it in a rodent- and insect-proof container. Keep the supply rotating during the good times.

- If your pet is on any medications, make sure you have a year's supply on hand.

- Try also to lay in a stock of veterinary antibiotics, anti-nausea and anti-diarrhea medicines, and others recommended by your vet. Some of these can also be used for humans. It's illegal, but cheaper than human medicine and may be necessary in a pinch. However, some animal medicines can hurt you. If you're discreet and on good terms with your vet, he or she might help you learn which are which. If not, check the *Physicians' Desk Reference* and other drug resource books on your library's reference shelves. Keep your pet's medicine in a cool, dark, dry place and remember to rotate new medicines in, as drugs lose their potency over time.

- Make sure all your pet's vaccinations are always current. The last thing you need is for Old Yeller to go rabid on you when everything else has already gone wrong.

- If you believe you might be forced to hit the road, think about what you'd need to take your animal friend with you — leashes, bedding, dishes, food, medicine, toys — and how your critter would get exercise or do its business if you were forced to hide out somewhere.

Last but not least, Mom, Dad, Grandma and Grandpa
In some ways, preparing your aging relatives for hard times is similar to preparing your kids. Like children, some old people will die rather than eat unfamiliar or unpleasant foods.

As with children, the stubborn crankiness of some old people can cause real problems in emergency situations.

It's going to vary a lot from family to family. Here are some things you might need to consider:

- Medicines. As you do for pets and kids, you'll need to lay in a supply of any regularly needed medications and rotate them so they'll still be good when you need them.
- Be sure to keep a good supply of their favorite foods on hand, particularly highly digestible ones like oatmeal.
- Realize you might have to cope with an old person's extreme resistance to change. To the best of your ability, keep familiar objects and people around and try to explain reasons for change.
- Resistance to change, crankiness, fussy eating and every other trait of aging could be hugely compounded if your aging relative is — or becomes — senile.
- As with children and pets, an old person can hamper you badly if you have to hit the road. Are your parents in good enough shape to survive on their own? If not, do you know someone who can care for them in your absence?
- I realize I'm buying into some stereotypes here, assuming your relatives' age will be a problem. If your family members are healthy and strong, consider that their age and experience might be an asset. A grandfather who fought in World War II might have valuable knowledge of fighting techniques. A great-aunt born on a farm during the Depression might be able to help with food storage and preparation, as well as other cheap-living techniques.
- Even if your parents or grandparents are healthy now, death is inevitable and long-term disability is extremely likely. Medicare and Social Security may not be available when the time comes — or, you might reject them for

philosophical reasons. Realize you could end up paying all the bills for a lengthy illness and/or taking a very sick old person into your home. (In fact, if Medicare collapses, but the government stays in power, you can count on either the feds or the state *forcing* you to pay your relatives' bills and confiscating your assets if you do not. Something like that has already happened in Oregon.) Consider, among other things, looking into alternative forms of medicine and having your relative enroll in the local branch of the Neptune Society for low cost, pre-arranged cremation services. One final organization that might be able to help, if your beliefs permit, is the Hemlock Society, which teaches humane forms of suicide and assisted suicide. Contact them at P.O. Box 11830, Eugene, Oregon 97440, (voice) (503) 342-5748 or 1-800-247-7421, (fax) (503) 345-2751.

Necessity is the plea for every infringement of human freedom. It is the argument of tyrants; it is the creed of slaves.
— William Pitt the Younger, British prime minister

86. Avoid "bear bait" cars and other attention-getting vehicles.

Ever see a red Miata chugging along at the speed limit, while a boxy old sedan cruises past and leaves the sports car in the dust? Smart owners of little red or yellow sports cars know they can't get away with moves that owners of gray or brown sedans perform with ease. Cops are always on the lookout, and color and style attract their eyes before deeds do.

Maybe smart car owners don't buy red or yellow sports cars in the first place.

Smart car owners buy whatever type of vehicle will be least noticeable in their environment.

For instance, if you're a tax resister or a member of the underground economy, you won't go running around in a Mercedes or Lexus that screams, "I have money!" If you live in a neighborhood of gardener-tended lawns and strict covenants, you won't drive around in a 1971 Chevy with the back window covered with duct tape and plastic wrap, either.

It *is* a matter of environment, though. I know of one Chicago resident who came to the attention of police in part because he drove around in a camo-painted jeep. In my neck of the woods, on the other hand (which literally is the *woods*), no one would even notice a camo paint job, or if they did, they'd just assume you were a hunter.

That little bland sedan box works pretty well wherever you go. These days, so does a small, dull-colored pickup truck or sport utility vehicle (sans running lights, roll bars and excess chrome, please!).

Of course you have a *right* to buy the vehicle of your choice. Of course you have a *right* to express yourself via bright paint jobs, camo or highly opinionated bumper stickers. Nobody's disputing that. The thing here is: don't call attention to yourself without thinking clearly about what you're doing. If you want a car or truck that shouts, "Here I am!" don't be surprised when cops, IRS agents and other people respond, "There you are."

Remember, vehicles are prime targets for civil forfeiture now. The better your car, the more likely some corrupt local or federal cop department is to take it from you on phony pretenses. Don't forget — these days when they take your property because they've caught you with drugs, a prostitute, "too much" cash — or whatever other "crime" they can cook up as an excuse—they don't have to prove your guilt in order to keep your car; *you* have to prove your innocence — and post a big, fat bond for the privilege of being allowed to try.

It is not a man's duty, as a matter of course, to devote himself to the eradication of any, even the most enormous wrong...But it is his duty...not to give it his practical support. If I devote myself to other pursuits and contemplations, I must first see, at least, that I do not pursue them sitting upon another man's shoulders.
    — Henry David Thoreau

87. Find a non-government occupation

With a few exceptions (discussed elsewhere), people who love freedom shouldn't be working for the government. Surprisingly, a lot do.

Or maybe it isn't surprising. Government has become so big a part of our lives that more than 50 percent of all U.S. households (closer to 60, actually) receive some form of government check every month — whether from employment, "entitlement," grant, loan, subsidy or something else.

If you work for the government, consider getting out. No matter how useful your job, you're being paid with stolen — taxed — money.

Then there are those of us who don't work for the government—but who really do, when you look closely at our jobs.

You also "work for the government" if:

- Your company sells its services chiefly to government agencies
- Your company markets a product primarily directed at the government market

- You are a tax accountant
- You are an attorney handling corporate regulatory affairs
- You are a human resources employee, or you work in areas such as "diversity" training, or the Americans With Disabilities Act, which involve government-mandated activities
- You spend a lot of your time filling out paperwork for the EPA or any other regulatory agency
- Your company makes a product that, though marketed to the private sector, would not have to exist if the government didn't require it

I'm not saying every one of these jobs, or even any of these jobs is "bad." Tax accountants do what they can to save clients from the worst the IRS has to offer. Environmental managers at factories do good by cutting down on pollution and health hazards, completely aside from the EPA's dictates. Corporate attorneys help keep corporations from being driven out of business by regulations and related lawsuits.

What I'm doing is simply asking you to be conscious of how much of your life might be devoted to working with or for the government without you particularly being aware of it, day to day. If it bothers you to be helping enforce government regulations or to know that half your income really comes from tax money, no matter that a private company issues the check, consider moving to some other type of work.

Ideally, independence

The ideal work has no dependence on government money at all. That's tough to find these days, but when you can find it, you may also discover it has bonuses. Non-government-involved jobs tend to be the smaller, more humane, much more independent ones such as:

- Gardener
- Self-employed carpenter
- Freelance writer
- Craft artist
- Printer
- Gunsmith
- Ranch hand
- Artist
- Video producer
- Restaurant owner
- Bed & breakfast operator
- Motel owner
- Independent plumber or electrician
- Upholsterer
- Cabinet-maker
- Veterinarian
- Chiropractor
- Retail-store owner
- Avon or Amway dealer
- Vending machine route owner
- Mechanic
- Welder
- Hairdresser
- Bicycle repairman
- Computer consultant
- Independent software engineer
- Tattoo artist
- Wood-lot operator
- Florist
- Truck owner-operator
- Picture framer
- Pet groomer

- Physician
- Security guard
- Independent mental-health counselor
- Fitness trainer
- Dentist
- Name a hundred more

A few of these occupations are, of course, still heavily regulated by the government (like trucking). A few aren't easy to earn a living at, but all are useful skills, with a minimum of daily government interference.

Better yet, some are ideal for practicing in a free economy. That means ideal for practicing in the tax-free underground economy now, and practicing in the more open free economy that could come later — either after an economic collapse or war... or perhaps even after we have set ourselves free.

On that day, this country will have a lot more use for florists, veterinarians and plumbers than for tax accountants and specialists in politically correct corporate policies.

Our forefathers made one mistake. What they should have fought for was representation without taxation.
— Fletcher Knebel, historian

88. Never beg for your rights

Free people *never* beg governments for fundamental rights like free speech, freedom of association, self-defense, worship and freedom to travel.

If the government gets in the way of your ability to live your life peacefully, as you see fit, in voluntary relationships with others, then it's wrong and you're right. Period.

Don't sit around and wait for Congress or the state legislature to "fix" violated rights. The very essence of the government game is that legislators give you a tiny bit *here* while grabbing a double handful of what's yours *there*. Even if you gain a victory or two, in the long run, government is a game freedom lovers can only lose.

Never, never beg or negotiate for your rights. Take them. If enough of us do, no government in the world can stand in our way.

> *The State is not armed with superior wit or honesty, but with superior physical strength. I was not born to be forced. I will breathe air after my own fashion. Let us see who is the strongest.*
> — Henry David Thoreau

89. Make "them" fill out your paperwork

Let bureaucrats know how it feels! Exercise your right to find out who your public servants are and where they derive their authority. When confronted with one of their many arrogant requests, politely hand them a copy of the "Bureaucracy Encounter Form," created by Charles Curley and yours truly to use to your heart's content:

The Bureaucracy Encounter Form

Dear Bureaucrat:

You have requested certain information or action of me. In order for me to better facilitate your request, I require certain information for my own records. If you will fill out this form in triplicate, I will then consider your request. Fill out a separate form for each request you have made of me. If additional room is needed, please use another sheet of paper.

Today's date __/__/__ Location: _____
Your name: _____
Agency(ies) you represent: _____

_____
Your business address: _____
City and state: _____
Postal code: _____
Telephone number: _____
Your annual salary: _____
Your supervisor's name: _____
Supervisor's telephone number: _____
Describe your request in detail: _____

_____
Are you required to make this request? _____
If so, what person or agency required it of you?_____

_____
Please state what statute, and what section and/or subsection
of that statute authorizes you to make this request: _____

_____
Please state which portion of the state or national constitution
authorizes you to make this request: _____

_____
Have you filled out a form like this for me in the past? ____
When? Exact dates: _____
What will be done with the information you collect? _____

_____
Is this part of a criminal investigation? _____
Will this become part of a criminal investigation? _____
I swear (or affirm) under penalty of perjury that the foregoing
is true and correct. (sign) _____

*The Democrats are the ones who will give you a loan.
The Republicans are the ones who will guarantee you a
loan. The Libertarians are the ones who will leave you
alone.*
— Cal Ludeman, Minnesota state representative

90. If you must vote (part I)....

If you must vote, vote Libertarian. You can contact the
national party at:

Libertarian Party Headquarters
Watergate Office Building
2600 Virginia Avenue NW, Suite 100
Washington, DC 20037
voice: 1-800-682-1776 (membership line)
e-mail: hq@lp.org
Web site: http://www.lp.org/

I'm not saying the Libertarians are perfect. After all, the
current partyarchs actually thought it was a good idea to
move the party headquarters into the Watergate building. (It
would be a much better idea to set up HQ in Midwest,
Wyoming, then loudly dare Washington DC to get off its elite
ass and get out in the real country.)

Still, if you have to vote at all, the LP beats the hell out of
the alternatives. There are party affiliates in all 50 states and
some counties. Headquarters can put you in touch.

*Always vote for a principle, though you vote alone,
and you may cherish the sweet reflection that your vote
is never lost.*
— John Quincy Adams

91. Get to know your neighbors

Who are those people living next door or across the street? Too often, these days, we don't really know. In a way, there's nothing wrong with not knowing; after all mere physical proximity doesn't mean you have a damn thing in common. Your neighbors could be nose-pickers, psychopaths or even Democrats.

Be that as it may, it behooves you to know something about the people around you, while nevertheless keeping your own reserve and privacy. Could these people be your allies in a political battle? Might they be good trading partners in an economic crisis — or people you could hire in the underground economy right now? Might they hire you? Is it possible they could help you homeschool your children?

On the other hand, if they're IRS agents, drug warriors or freelance busybodies, you might want to know that, too. (Not that anyone would admit to working for the IRS, but you can find out over time.)

In any case, it never hurts to make their acquaintance, then maintain it at a cordial distance if that's what suits you.

The simple step of a courageous individual is not to take part in the lie. One word of truth outweighs the world.
— Alexander Solzhenitsyn

92. Network—but wisely and discreetly

My honey and I attend meetings of an influential conservative group, held in the private meeting room of a restaurant. We aren't conservatives (as you might have guessed!), but these guys are impressive, we like the leaders very much, and we learn a lot from them about how to accomplish goals. Their meetings often attract people from other groups, seeking alliances.

One day, about a year ago, a cammie-clad stranger showed up, stood up, introduced himself as a militia leader from another county, handed around literature, and announced that he was stockpiling guns and food and that anyone with half a brain would be doing the same. He gave his name, home address and home phone number to anyone who requested it.

Later, after the general meeting, a couple of us spoke briefly to him in the public area of the crowded restaurant. With no context, he abruptly announced that he was prepared to defend himself at any time, pulled up his jacket to reveal a .38, and announced it was "okay" because he had a concealed carry permit.

We were not surprised when, a few months later, we learned his militia group had fallen apart. He said it was because they were cowards, scared off after the Oklahoma City bombing. He had no idea it was probably because he was a complete fool.

You can easily see some of his mistakes. He was blatting out information that was: 1) nobody's business; and, 2) could have endangered himself and his associates.

But his equally serious error was that he was so wrapped up in himself that he forgot to "learn the territory."

He didn't realize — because he didn't go through the long, careful process of finding out — that the group to which he was speaking contained some very wise, and very sensible, people.

He didn't learn there were already two other leaders of militia-type organizations present. He didn't understand that at least a third of the men in the room, and several of the women, were also armed (with or without permit), and would hardly be impressed by his rooster-like display of weapons.

He didn't understand that these people were smart enough to realize that anyone blurting out his own secret plans would just as quickly blurt out theirs.

Above all, he didn't take the time to discover that these people were, for the most part, more knowledgeable than he about the things he was so insistent on "teaching" them.

He was so clueless and so arrogant I've often wondered if he was an undercover cop.

It's important to build alliances, and to learn what other groups of potential allies (and potential enemies) are doing. But you've got to use some sense about it:

- Take the time to find out who others are before you reveal much about yourself.
- Never, ever reveal more than you have to.
- Even after you think you know some other individual or group, always hold a tiny bit of suspicion in your heart.
- Have an address and phone number that doesn't give every nut and goon a roadmap to your house.
- When trying to forge alliances, respect the other person's intelligence; though the nation is filled with TV-anesthetized zombies, politically aware people are, these days, *very* aware.

"If the law supposes that," said Mr. Bumble..., "the law is a ass — a idiot."
— Charles Dickens, *Oliver Twist*

93. Intimidate back

When some pompous authority figure is "pomping" bullshit all over you, mutter remarks like, "My attorney doesn't see it that way..." or, "Interesting. That's not what the governor told me..." or, "Not according to Title III of the state code."

You can usually count on bureaucrats being either stupid or lazy. If they weren't, they'd have real jobs, doing something useful. Even if they continue blustering at you, you will have planted a seed of doubt. Because of their laziness, they'll almost never go to the trouble to disprove your mumbling. You will regain the offensive and give them a little dose of fear.

It may be better to live under robber barons than under omnipotent moral busybodies. The robber baron's cruelty may sometimes sleep, his cupidity may at some point be satisfied; but those who torment us for our own good will torment us without end, for they do so with the approval of their own conscience.
— C.S. Lewis

94. Know when — and whether — you could kill

In a way, this isn't fair. People who've been there say it isn't possible to know whether you could kill until you've been placed in that position. About all they say for sure is that those who brag most loudly about their own ruthless bravery are the ones most likely to pee their pants and run.

Nevertheless, it's a subject you need to think about as part of your preparedness.

Try picturing yourself in various scenarios: a thug kicks down your door in the middle of the night; a rapist stalks you down a lonely street; soldiers come door-to-door in your neighborhood, looking for "contraband" guns; you are alone in the woods, being tracked by cops on a trumped up charge; your ex-partner, in a rage, charges at you with a baseball bat.

Now don't imagine yourself as Rambo or James Bond, coolly out-thinking every enemy. Get real. It's cold and wet in those woods. You're exhausted and not thinking well after

36 hours without sleep. You don't know who's kicking your door in. You're terrified and your heart's pumping like a gusher. You can't remember whether you left a round in the chamber. Somebody's screaming, "Freeze!!! Police!!!" but for all you know they could be freelance gangsters instead of real cops. Or they could be real cops, come to kill you or carry you to an internment camp. You know that trailing stranger behind you outweighs you by 50 pounds — but you don't know if he's really stalking you or not.

In seconds, you have moral choices, strategic choices, philosophical choices all screaming to be made NOW.

Think about how you're going to feel if that intruder in the night turns out to be nothing more than the guy from the next apartment, opening the wrong door. What if it's a 13-year-old kid? What if those black-clad, face-masked gangsters really were cops, after all?

Think about somebody's brains on your carpet, about the smell of a gut shot, about the lawsuits and legal charges that might wreck the rest of your life.

Now, do you think you could kill? Under which circumstances? And do you need more preparation (self-defense classes, practical shooting experience, knowledge of military tactics, etc.) to help you face what may, someday, be the decision of your life?

95. If you must vote (part II)...

If you've absolutely got to go to the polls... and if there are no Libertarians on the ballot... or if you don't like them any better than the Republicrats, Laborites, Socialist Workers, Natural Law folks or whatever, then write in:

- Mickey Mouse
- Dan Rostenkowski
- Richard Nixon

- Attila the Hun
- Yourself
- Your dog Dingleberry
- Thomas Jefferson
- Randy Weaver
- Ted Kaczynsky
- Ted Bundy
- Dilbert
- Henry David Thoreau
- Joe Camel
- Mary Juana
- Samuel Colt
- or None of the Above

In other words: send a message, waste somebody's time, let them know the whole voting business is pabulum to keep the citizens appeased, and you're on to the game.

You lucky folks in Nevada can even vote for None of the Above without having to write him, her or it in. Too bad the vote cops still have it rigged so that if None wins, a politician-as-usual still gets to put his or her backside in the chair of office.

We, the people, are the rightful masters of both Congress and the courts — not to overthrow the Constitution, but to overthrow men who pervert the Constitution.
— Abraham Lincoln

96. Learn your privacy rights and protect them

In a way, this whole book is about privacy rights. When you carry a gun without a permit, refuse to give your Social Security number, don't answer nosy questions, place your

Visa card records out of reach, bury gold and silver, encrypt your electronic transmissions, and generally live a low-profile life, you're taking steps to guard your privacy.

But as with civil forfeiture and "gun control" (really victim control), this is an area where the attack from outside is so intense, and increasing so greatly, you may need to do more than merely take care of yourself. You need to join and support the organizations that are fighting the public battle.

Everybody talks about the increasing invasion of privacy. This is one threat to freedom the mainstream media even deigns to mention occasionally! But not too many organizations are actually doing much about it.

And, as usual, our rulers, while decrying "government on our backs," are rushing to pass laws to make matters worse. As I write this, proposals for a national I.D. card are very much alive in Congress, along with a system by which employers would be required to get permission from the federal government before hiring anyone — giving the feds yet one more database with which to track and manipulate your life.

It isn't only government that's putting the clamps on you. Businesses may be the biggest culprit — from the credit card companies that track every purchase you make (and sell information on your buying habits to yet other nosy businesses!), to employers who imagine they have a right to know whether you practice "unhealthy" or illegal habits on your own time. Of course, all information collected by businesses is ultimately available to fedsnoops, as well, by subpoena, warrant, force or deception.

What to do about it

First, there are the personal things we've already been talking about. Do those and learn to do more. (As usual, Loompanics has a good supply of books on the subject.)

Two good books on the political background and personal implications of privacy loss are:

- *Our Vanishing Privacy: And What You Can Do to Protect Yours*, by Robert Ellis Smith, Loompanics Unlimited, 1993.
- *War Stories: Accounts of Persons Victimized by Invasions of Privacy*, by Robert Ellis Smith, *Privacy Journal*, 1993.

Smith is the publisher of *Privacy Journal*, which publishes good (though entirely mainstream) information and could lead you to organizations and resources to help protect your privacy — and everyone else's.

Privacy Journal
Box 28577
Providence, Rhode Island 02908
(401) 274-7861
Web site: http://www.epic.org/priv_journ.html

Try also:

Privacy Times
Box 21501
Washington, DC 20009
voice: (202) 829-3660
fax: (202) 829-3653
e-mail: privtime@access.digex.net

Neither of these magazines is cheap. *Privacy Journal* runs about $125 per year, and $225 for *Privacy Times*, but if you're interested in keeping abreast, there they are.

There are dozens of other books on privacy issues. Among them are:

- *The Privacy Act*, by Grant Liddell, Oxford University Press, 1995.
- *Privacy in America: Is Your Private Life in the Public Eye?*, by David F. Linowes, University of Illinois Press, 1989.
- *Privacy as a Constitutional Right: Sex, Drugs and the Right to Life*, by Darian A. McWhirter and Jon D. Bible, Quorum Books, 1992.
- *Mind Your Own Business: The Battle for Personal Privacy*, by Gini Graham and Ph. D. Scott, Plenum Press, 1995.

I've found only one "public interest" organization dedicated to informing people of their privacy rights. It's specifically for Californians, and it focuses primarily on consumer issues, but it could be helpful to anyone. It is:

The Privacy Rights Clearinghouse
Center for Public Interest Law
University of San Diego School of Law
5998 Alcala Park
San Diego, CA 92110-2492
Telephone: (619) 260-4806
Fax: (619) 260-4753
Hotline: 1-800-773-7748 (California only)
Hotline: (619) 298-3396 (non-California residents)

It publishes these fact sheets:
- Privacy Survival Guide
- Cordless and Cellular Phones: Is Everybody Listening?

- How to Put an End to Harassing Phone Calls
- Junk Mail: How Did They All Get My Address?
- Telemarketing: Whatever Happened to a Quiet Evening at Home?
- How Private Is My Credit Report?
- Employee Monitoring: Is There Privacy in the Workplace?
- How Private Is My Medical Information?
- Wiretapping and Eavesdropping: Is There Cause for Concern?
- My Social Security Number: How Secure Is It?
- From Cradle to Grave: Government Records and Your Privacy
- A Checklist of Responsible Information-Handling Practices
- Are You Being Stalked? Tips for Prevention
- Paying By Credit Card or Check: What Can Merchants Ask?
- Employment Background Checks: A Jobseeker's Guide

The clearinghouse also does research on privacy issues and supplies it to legislators, think tanks and consumer groups.

I hate to say it, but the one organization that appears to be most effectively engaged in the public battle against the loss of privacy is the American Civil Liberties Union. I hesitate to recommend joining this group, which has always been *very* selective about which parts of the Bill of Rights it chooses to support, and which invents group "rights" by whim to replace individual ones. So I will just say, check it out:

American Civil Liberties Union
132 West 43rd Street
New York, New York 10036-6599
Web site: http://www.aclu.org

The ACLU has published a handbook: *Your Right to Privacy: A Basic Guide to Legal Rights in an Information Society,* by Evan Hendricks, et al.

Whether you join or not, you can download issue papers on topics such as these from their Web site:

* Privacy of medical records
* Workers' privacy rights
* Government secrecy
* Cyberliberties and other telecommunications issues
* Censorship
* Gay/lesbian issues
* AIDS/HIV
* Wiretapping

In one recent, strongly worded report, the ACLU said the FBI's latest proposals for snooping "would make the KGB look like privacy advocates." So these guys aren't all bad, even if they aren't all good, either.

> *This country, with its institutions, belongs to the people who inhabit it. Whenever they shall grow weary of the existing government, they can exercise their constitutional right of amending it, or the revolutionary right to dismember or overthrow it.*
>   — Abraham Lincoln

97. Bury gold, guns and goodies

You know by now that paranoia is good for your health. One of the healthiest ways to express paranoia is to bury guns, gold, silver and other goodies that might be: 1) illegal; and, 2) desperately necessary in times of crisis.

Do not bury them on your own property. If your stash is found by government agents, everything you own could be instantly forfeited if the stash contains a single item that violates certain laws or regulations.

Bury them on:

- National forest land or Bureau of Land Management lands
- The property of someone you hate
- The property of a politician or bureaucrat

In the west, where the feds kept most of the land for themselves, national forest land and BLM land is easy to find. If you live in the east, which was settled before government decided it could get away with owning half of a state, try a remote corner of a state park. Make sure the site you choose is:

- Easy to find again
- So remote that no one else is likely to see you digging the hole or accidentally stumble upon your stash
- Restored to its original condition once you've covered the hole

Items you might want to bury:

- Guns. Especially guns. Especially military-style rifles like an SKS (if you're on a budget) or an M1 Garand (if you care enough to bury the very best). Perhaps also a reliable but relatively inexpensive handgun, like one of Ruger's line of "P" and "KP" semi-autos.
- Ammo.
- Emergency money. This might include a mixture of Federal Reserve Notes, pre-1964 U.S. silver coins, and gold (either in the form of Canadian Maple Leaves or South African Krugerands, one ounce or ½ ounce). You need a variety of types of money, since you can't anticipate the economic situation you might face. If FRNs

haven't been inflated into toilet paper, they'll be your easiest source of spending cash. However, if your FRNs have become obsolete, worthless or illegal, pre-1964 silver coins (with real silver, not pot metal like modern coins) will always be negotiable. You'll be able to rely on the coin's face value, and probably on its greater metal value. Gold, of course, has always been considered real money and, while not useful for quick spending, can always be negotiated somewhere, somehow.

• Emergency food and water. Enough to last for a few days. Items packaged for long-term storage, like military meals-ready-to-eat and foil packets of water from an emergency store are best.

• Other small items you anticipate needing in your particular circumstances like: compass, map, solar/crank operated radio, firestarters, sleeping bag, spare eyeglasses, chemicals, etc.

Unless you have lots of money, time, space and a master plan, this stash will necessarily have to be fairly small. So choose your items carefully.

Then bury them in such a way that they are protected against moisture, animals, prying eyes, and pressure of the soil above them.

If you can also protect them against discovery via metal detectors, sound waves or infrared, so much the better. One nice way to get around both metal detectors and aerial surveillance is to dig your stash under an old abandoned auto or refrigerator. Choose one that's been there forever and looks likely to remain that way. Then, unless the searchers really, really have reason to suspect your stash is there, they won't bother with what looks (and sounds, to their equipment) like nothing but a derelict hulk.

Special instructions for burying guns

   Guns are one of the trickiest things to stash, since "sweating" of underground moisture into their container, coupled with faint exhalations of moisture from the objects themselves, can ruin metal and mechanical parts within months. Here's one way to protect them:

1. Start with a length of six- or eight-inch diameter plastic pipe, available from any wholesale plumbing supply. You may have to buy it in 20-foot lengths or some other fixed dimension, but you can have that cut into your desired shorter lengths.

2. Purchase caps to seal each end of the tube. There are two basic types of end caps — threaded ones, designed to be removable, and non-threaded ones, designed to seal the end of the pipe permanently. Threaded caps are expensive! And to use them you'll either need to affix a threaded nipple to the end of the tube or buy pipe pre-threaded. If you want repeated access to the goodies in the tube, you'll appreciate threaded end caps. If you plan to crack open your stash only once, get the other kind.

3. Seal one end of the tube, using a permanent cap, held in place by epoxy or another glue/sealant recommended by the tube's supplier.

4. Disassemble your guns and coat all parts thoroughly with a thick layer of wheel-bearing grease. Many other water-resistant coatings will do, but wheel-bearing grease works as well as any, is cheaper than most, and can be wiped off with a cloth when you need your weapons — no fancy solvents required.

5. Line the inside of the tube with disposable diapers. These absorb moisture and have the additional advantage of having a layer that "keeps the moisture away from baby's delicate skin" — or the delicate metal of your guns.

6. Lay the disassembled and coated gun parts on the diapers. You can wrap the parts *lightly* in plastic or cheesecloth if you wish, but make sure there are plenty of breathing holes in any plastic or other non-permeable material you choose. Otherwise, all you're doing is trapping moisture next to the metal, defeating your other anti-corrosion precautions.

7. Add a bag or bags of desiccant material for extra security against moisture. Desiccants are substances that absorb moisture from their surroundings and trap it inside their cells. The silica gel that comes packed in little bags with cameras, computers and some dried survival foods is a good desiccant. (That's what it's there for.) If you've been saving those gel packets, great. If not, your local camera or computer shop might have bags and bags of it you can beg or buy. For a cheap, easily available emergency desiccant, try uncooked white rice. It, too, absorbs moisture and traps it, but I don't know enough about the long-term properties of rice to recommend it as a permanent solution.

8. Seal the open end of the tube. If you've chosen a threaded end cap, first spread a ring of grease around the edge of the pipe to help seal the connection between tube and cap. Then wrap Teflon tape around the threads on the tube before you screw the cap on. Teflon tape, also available from your pipe supplier, has two purposes: it helps seal against moisture, and it will make it easier to open a long-sealed, long-buried cache. Finally, spread another thick layer of grease around the outside edge where the tube and cap meet, again, to guard against moisture getting in. For extra security, you could use epoxy, Lok-Tite or some other glue/sealant around the outside edge of the cap, to seal the minute gap between

cap and tube; just make sure it's something you can peel off, chip off or dissolve — easily and quickly! — when the time comes. If you've chosen a permanent end cap, affix it as you did the first cap — but again making sure you can break through the sealant or otherwise crack open the tube when you need what's inside.

9. Now bury it in a safe spot, several feet deep. Bury it below the frost line for your area, in order to keep the plastic from being squeezed and cracked by ice. That means burying it deeper than four feet in a climate like Wisconsin's or Maine's and more than three feet in most parts of Colorado, Kansas or the mid-Atlantic states. On the west coast or in the south, you should still bury it several feet deep, for security reasons, even if the negligible frost in your climate doesn't demand it. Burying it this deep makes it more difficult to access, especially in winter when the ground is frozen. But for long-term storage, this is the only way to prevent damage to the tube and its contents.

10. Be sure you give yourself a good way of remembering where your stash is, but if you write the instructions down, make sure they're coded in such a way that only you, or a chosen few relatives or associates, can interpret them.

Important Note: You can purchase ready-made cache tubes from suppliers who occasionally place ads in the back of publications like *Soldier of Fortune* or *Guns and Ammo*. Please keep in mind the possibility that these companies could be BATF or FBI front organizations, designed to catch people exactly like you. Even if they are legitimate companies, you cannot assume their mailing lists will remain confidential.

98. Maybe you're already a "terrorist"

Remember, this is not the America we learned about in school. Under the Clinton Terror bill, the federal government can declare any organization to be "terrorist," for any reason. The government is not required to reveal its reasons or present any evidence at all to support its claim. There is no appeal process. Once the feds have declared any group to be "terrorist," its mailing lists and other records are turned over to the government. Anyone who ever made a donation or purchased goods from the organization is now a federal criminal. If you even bought tickets to a concert sponsored by an organization the government doesn't like, you can be sent to federal prison — or at least harassed and investigated.

So before you order a caching tube, donate to a cause, purchase firearm equipment by mail, or do anything else that is — or might ever be considered — politically incorrect, THINK!

Contribute or place orders by cash or money order only. Use a false name and an address that does not lead directly to you (like a general delivery address, or a private mailbox rented under someone else's name).

Don't stop contributing to organizations or buying the supplies you need. It's more important than ever to keep doing these things! Just understand that, even if your life is presently peaceful and seemingly secure, the machinery of tyranny and the laws to implement tyranny are already in place. It's only a matter of time until the federal government chooses to use them to smash all dissent.

No man escapes when freedom fails
The best men rot in filthy jails.
And those who cried, "Appease! Appease!"
Are hanged by those they tried to please.
— Author unknown

99. Put a warning sign on your property

You can let gov-o-crats, from the local tax assessor to fedgoons, know exactly where you stand, and where *they* stand, before they enter your property.

Something like this, posted on your door or on a gate to your land, might do the trick:

NOTICE

To all government agents, city, county, state and federal, of any and all agencies:

This property and its inhabitants are under the protection of the Bill of Rights.

Government agents entering herein are obligated to obey all provisions of said bill.

Your particular attention is called to Amendments II and IV:

II: A well-regulated militia being necessary to the security of a free State, the right of the people to keep and bear arms shall not be infringed.

IV: The right of the people to be secure in their persons, houses, papers, and effects against unreasonable searches and seizures shall not be violated, and no Warrants shall issue, but upon probable cause, supported by Oath or affirmation, and

particularly describing the place to be searched, and the
persons or things to be seized.

Entry to this property will be allowed only with a properly
drawn and signed warrant, reviewed by the occupants and/or
their attorney at time of entry.

You could leave off the Second Amendment, if you aren't
a gun owner, don't want to advertise your gun ownership, or
don't care to appear "threatening." The crux of the message
is Amendment IV, anyway.

The line about showing the warrant is mainly a demand for
courtesy; the smash-and-grab variety of cop will ignore it, but
it informs more sensible cops and bureaucrats that you will
treat them decently if they treat you decently.

A notice such as this will call attention to you, of course.
But it might also protect you after the fact of an illegal search
and seizure. Federal law provides penalties for those who
violate your constitutional rights "under color of law." The
fact that the entering agents saw your sign is evidence,
useable in court, that they were aware of the rights they were
violating.

*Universally, instinctively, individuals hate and fear the
state. The staunchest, most paternalistic conservative,
the most intrusively maternalistic liberal, each
blanches at a phone call from the government's
collection agency and palpitates for hours afterward,
no matter how sincerely he advocates coercive politics
at other times or tries to comply with the letter and
spirit of the law. Should either ever acquire the
integrity to realize what this means, and the courage to
do something about it, the world will change
materially for the better.*
— L. Neil Smith, *Pallas*

100. If you can risk it, don't pay income taxes

Opponents of the federal income tax make various arguments against it:

- That filing violates our Fifth Amendment right against self-incrimination;
- That the 16th Amendment, that gave us the income tax, was never properly ratified by the states;
- That taxation violates our Fourth Amendment rights against unreasonable seizure;
- That only corporations and others that receive privileges from government are actually required by law to pay;
- That wages, being simply a trade of time for money, are not "income" (defined as unearned money, such as stock dividends);
- That only certain types of citizens are required to pay;
- That the IRS says taxation is voluntary, and we therefore have a right not to "volunteer";
- That (because of Fifth Amendment concerns) there is actually no law requiring individuals to file a tax return, and the IRS relies on fuzzy wording and intimidation to disguise the fact that the law was never even written.

If you've studied the matter, you may have concluded that several of these are damn fine arguments. I agree. The Fifth Amendment argument is impeccable, as long as you consider the income tax a punishment for making money. The argument that "wages" are not "income" sounds strange until you realize that, at the time the tax was sold to the public as a soak-the-rich scheme, wages were *not* taxed and work-for-hire was indeed, rightly, seen as a straight-across trade, without taxable gain. The wage tax was introduced to finance World War II, and we've obviously been paying for that war ever since.

The more you read and study these issues, the more you find that a stunning number of them have at least some validity, popular conceptions to the contrary.

But whatever you think of the merits of these arguments, they all beg the point. As good or feeble as they may be, there is really one reason above all to resist the income tax:

- Because I am not a slave. What I earn belongs, by right, to me. I may gladly purchase government services if they are offered on the open market. Or I may reject them if I find them useless, inadequate or offensive. But no institution on this earth has the ·uthority to claim my labor, my time and my life as its right. These things belong to me, now and forever.

Then there is the secondary, but still vital, consideration that the most effective way to bring down a corrupt, abusive government is to cut off the flow of money into its maw.

We can fight and fight and fight for freedom, but as long as we continue to feed the destroyer of freedom, we are fighting against ourselves.

But what to do about it?

Because this is a decision that can cost you everything — your property, your freedom, your dignity, your money, your reputation, your job, your family, and even your life — no one could presume to say, "You should stop paying right now."

It's easy if you're single without kids to support. It's easy if you're self-employed and don't have the feds taking their bite week-by-week with your employer's help. It's easy if you don't have much in the first place and know the IRS probably wouldn't bother persecuting you. It's easy if you've reached a point in life where you believe you'd truly rather die than live as a slave.

But no matter how hard it is, you've still got to keep coming back to the same points: Am I free or a slave? Can I, in conscience, feed this monster at the same time I struggle to subdue it?

If you want to opt out, you could take the Thoreau/Ayn Rand approach and simply "go on strike." You could say, *"Non serviam* — I will not serve you any longer." I will live my life despite you. My freedom does not depend on your actions.

You can also continue to file, but voluntarily lower your income to deny the feds (or the state) the product of your productivity. If you're interested in that approach, several of the books listed in *Read: self-reliance,* No. 48, can help you live on less.

Or you could read, study, and take one of the more legalistic approaches offered by some of the better known tax resisters. These often involve filing various forms of paperwork declaring yourself not subject to the tax. There have recently been a few high-profile criminal tax cases won on this basis. One of these was the Lloyd Long case. Long was charged with two counts of willful failure to file his federal income taxes in 1989 and 1990. A federal court found him not guilty on either count, on the basis of his argument that he did not consider himself required to pay. The case is United States of America vs. Lloyd R. Long, Case number CR-1-93-91, in the U.S. District Court for the Eastern District of Tennessee, Chattanooga. You should be able to obtain copies of the transcript from one of Long's attorneys, the well-known defender of freedom cases, Lowell Becraft at:

Lowell H. (Larry) Becraft, Jr., Esq.
Attorney at Law
209 Lincoln Street
Huntsville, Alabama 35801

Web site:

http://www.logoplex.com/resources/becraft/becraft.html, or:

Eric Gray
e-mail: eric-ucc1-207@usa.net
Web site: http://freedombyfaith.com

Anyone who presumes to insist you stop paying the income tax is indeed presumptuous — and possibly hazardous to your health, as well. But if you want to find out more for yourself about various methods available, here are some places to investigate:

Irwin Schiff
Freedom Books
620 S. 11th St. #7
Las Vegas, Nevada 89101
1-800-829-6666 (book order number)
e-mail: ischiff@ix.netcom.com
Web site: http://www.ischiff.com

A noted tax resister and seminar speaker, Schiff is the author of *How Anyone Can Stop Paying Taxes* and other books on taxation and federal "funny money." Be aware that most of Schiff's books were written in the late '70s and early '80s, and that Schiff himself spent time in prison for practicing what he preaches. (I don't think spending time in prison discredits Schiff anymore than it discredited Martin Luther King; but it does serve as a warning that his methods must be regarded with caution.)

Read *War Tax Resistance: A Guide to Withholding Your Support from the Military*, by Ed Hedemann and Ruth Benn. Whether or not you agree with the politics of the authors, you'll find useful advice here about resistance methods and IRS collection and appeal procedures.

Contact any of the sovereign citizen information sources listed in *Consider sovereign citizenship*, No. 63.

For more information about IRS methods, read *A Law Unto Itself: The IRS and the Abuse of Power*, by David Burnham, Vintage Books, New York, 1989.

If you just want to avoid taxes by avoiding coming to the IRS's notice, try *Guerrilla Capitalism*, by Adam Cash, Loompanics Unlimited, 1984. This book and its sequel, *How To Do Business "Off the Books,"* describe how to operate in the free market — which, in a controlled world like ours, means the underground economy. Be aware that these books are more than 10 years old, and that the IRS is constantly coming up with new rules and procedures to tighten the noose on free marketeers. With that in mind, there's still plenty of good advice here.

For what it's worth, I still think the best advice for resisting government can be found in Henry David Thoreau's famous essay, *On Civil Disobedience*. Thoreau went to jail (for a single night) for refusing to pay a tax. His essay reflects the philosophy, not of someone willing to battle the government using its own legalistic tools, but of someone who just says (as I interpret it), "The government and its doings are neither my concern nor my responsibility. If it knows what's good for it, it will stay out of my life."

When I meet a government which says to me, "Your money or your life," why should I be in haste to give it my money? It may be in a great strait, and not know what to do; I cannot help that. It must help itself; do as I do... I am not responsible for the successful working of the machinery of society.
— Henry David Thoreau

> *I still believe there is not a man in this country that can't make a living for himself and his family. But he can't make a living for them and his government, too. Not the way this government is living. What the government has got to do is live as cheap as the people.*
>
> — Will Rogers

101. Don't fire until you see the whites of their eyes

Someday, if we aren't able to turn the march of tyranny aside, there will be blood. Not just in Oklahoma City, or Waco or on Ruby Ridge, but everywhere.

Already, in the week I write this, bombs have either gone off or been discovered unexploded in three centers of patriot activity. In the last several months, bombs have gone off or been defused in Spokane, Washington, Reno, Nevada, rural Montana and Georgia. Or at least, so the media reports say.

Much as I understand the frustration of watching rights be legislated and regulated away... much as I understand the additional frustration of standing by numb and defeated as these violations pour forth from a Congress that pledged to "get government off our backs" ...much as mayhem and bloody revenge make satisfying fantasies, I just can't accept that this is the way to go.

We bring government's might down on the entire country when we strike — even when the strike is made with nothing but a pipe bomb of a sort any curious boy used to be free to make. (I'm *not* saying a pipe bomb is no big deal; it sure as hell is if you're standing next to it when it goes off. But a mugging, murder or rape is a big deal, too, to the victim; yet these crimes seldom provoke the wrath of the entire federal government. What I'm talking about here is gross over-reaction to deeds the feds view as defiance of their authority.)

Perhaps you could look at that as a positive strategy. The more we strike, the more government clamps down; the more it clamps down, the more ordinary people are driven to rebel; the more ordinary people rebel, the sooner tyranny falls.

But then, the fall is chaotic and catastrophic. Then we are all caught in it. Then, we may end up with an even worse tyranny in place of the one that collapsed.

These bombs and bombings are the work of the mine canaries. When the poison gasses build up in the shaft, the canaries carried down by the miners die first, giving the people a chance to get out. People who are reacting to tyranny with violence now are, indeed, reacting realistically. Just sooner than need be for the rest of us.

Or consider another possibility — that these alleged bombs and bombings were the work of the feds, trying to provoke or discredit us, or trying to get more laws passed that will rob us of our historic rights. Since this book first went to press, that's been confirmed in several cases. Fed informants built bombs or bought bomb parts, but their set-up victims went to prison anyway, just for talking about the possibility of violence. Or alleged "conspiracies" turned out to be much, much less than the media and the government announced. But, again, harmless people went to prison just for speaking unwisely or owning politically incorrect hardware. We do not yet have the strength or organization to win a conflict with government.

So when is the time for violence? I hope never. I'd rather we bring the "system" down by declaring our own freedom, then laughing at government as it flails and gnashes its teeth in an impotent effort to regain control.

On my optimistic days, I even think we could do it.

On days like today, when the Clinton Terror bill is too oppressive a reality, the national ID card is lurking in the background, the media remains silent as people's homes are seized without due process, and U.S. Marshals strut their awards of valor for shooting a child in the back, I don't think so.

What I do think, though, is that if the day comes when we must take back our freedom through violence, we will know it. It won't just be a few lonely militiamen in the woods who will see it. Thousands and hundreds of thousands of us will come to the same, inevitable conclusion.

It was Charles Fort who observed, "It steam-engines when it comes steam-engine time." He meant that, though there may be a long chain of events leading up to a discovery, an invention, or an event, the thing itself will not come to be until all conditions are right. Maybe it was one man's initiative, Robert Fulton's, to build the first steamboat, but he had to have Watt before him to explore steam power, a receptive shipping industry ahead of him to keep his invention alive, and a receptive intellectual climate all around him to foster his thinking.

In the fight for freedom, we are very near "steam-engine time." I think the only reason it hasn't happened already is that so many people are dependent on the government "massa" for their daily survival. But it will happen, one way or another.

It may be one person's initiative to aim the first effective strike. But we'll know when it's time to follow. At that moment, we'll "see the whites of their eyes." And at that moment, fire.

I do believe that where there is a choice only between cowardice and violence, I would advise violence.
        — Gandhi

Appendix I

Other sources for books and pamphlets of interest to libertarians and patriots are:

Liberty Tree Books
Independent Institute
134 Ninety-Eighth Avenue
Oakland, California 94603
voice: (510) 568-6047
1-800-927-8733
Web site: http://www.independent.org

International Society for Individual Liberty
1800 Market Street
San Francisco, California 94102
voice: (415) 864-0952
fax: (415) 864-7506
e-mail: 71034.2711@compuserve.com
Web site: http://www.isil.org

YOU WILL ALSO WANT TO READ:

☐ **10048 THE BIG BOOK OF SECRET HIDING PLACES,** *by Jack Luger.* This is the biggest and best book on concealment of physical objects ever printed! This book tells how searchers find hidden contraband and how to hide your stuff so it can't be found. Topics include: Hiding places in the home and the automobile; Tools and techniques used by searchers including mirrors, metal detectors, vapor detectors, dogs, and more. The different types of searchers you may encounter and the intensity of the searches they conduct; The tools you need to build your own secret hiding places and where to get them; How much work is involved; A lengthy chapter on concealing weapons and the best tactics for employing them. *1987, 8½ x 11, 128 pp, more than 100 illustrations, soft cover.* **$14.95**

☐ **10049 HOW TO BURY YOUR GOODS, The Complete Manual of Long-Term Underground Storage,** *by eddie the wire.* A completely illustrated guide to all the in's and out's of underground storage. Burial containers; Proper packaging; Protecting your site from discovery; Finding your site when you need your goods; Burying large machinery and gasoline; and Much More! You never know when you will need weapons, food and other survival items. *1987, 5½ x 8½, 72 pp, illustrated, soft cover.* **$8.00**

☐ **61147 HOW TO LEGALLY OBTAIN A SECOND CITIZENSHIP AND PASSPORT — AND WHY YOU WANT TO,** *by Adam Starchild.* An American citizenship and passport are two of the most highly-prized possessions a person can have... but there are distinct legal and financial advantages to having a *second* citizenship and passport. Author Adam Starchild explains the reasons and methods for acquiring both, in his highly-informative book. Covered are: A brief history of passports and nationality; How nationality is acquired; The advantages and disadvantages of multiple nationalities; How a second passport is obtained; Prerequisites for acquiring both a second citizenship and passport. *1995, 5½ x 8½, 131 pp, soft cover.* **$15.00**

To order any of the above titles or titles on the following pages by credit card, call 1-800-380-2230, 8am to 4pm, Monday through Friday or use the order form at the end of the book. Also see the catalog ad at the end of the book. **Our catalog is FREE with the purchase of any title listed, or $5.00 if sold separately.**

YOU WILL ALSO WANT TO READ:

☐ **17079 TRAVEL-TRAILER HOMESTEADING UNDER $5,000,** *by Brian Kelling.* Tired of paying rent? Need privacy away from nosy neighbors? This book will show how a modest financial investment can enable you to place a travel-trailer or other RV on a suitable piece of land and make the necessary improvements for a comfortable home in which to live! This book covers the cost break-down, tools needed, how to select the land and travel-trailer or RV, and how to install a septic system, as well as water, power (including solar panels), heat and refrigeration systems. Introduction by Bill Kaysing. *1995, 5½ x 8½, 80 pp, illustrated, indexed, soft cover.* **$8.00**

☐ **17025 VONU, The Search for Personal Freedom,** *by Rayo, Edited by Jon Fisher.* Rayo was an early pioneer of libertarian theory. He coined the term "vonu" (invulnerability to coercion) and discussed non-political means of achieving freedom here and now. This collection of articles draws on Rayo's experiences as a van nomad and wilderness dweller. Loaded with practical information on how to squat on public or private lands and live well in the wild. *1983, 5½ x 8½, 112 pp, illustrated, soft cover.* **$10.00**

☐ **85225 A MAN'S GUIDE TO ADVERTISING FOR A WOMAN,** *by Sebastian Phillips.* Men! Are your desperately seeking a woman... or would you like to? Then this book is a must! It explains how to properly structure "Personals" ads that will attract not *one*, but *many* women. Learn where, when and why to place your ads, buzzwords that get results, the do's and don'ts of composition, how to screen your responses, and how to stack the odds in your favor so that the war between the sexes comes to a screeching halt and love and courtship prevail! Contains never-before-published information on Internet ads, as well as informed details on magazines and newspaper advertising. This is the best book ever written on this subject. *1996, 5½ x 8½, 175 pp, illustrated, soft cover.* **$16.95**

To order any of the above titles or titles on the following pages by credit card, call 1-800-380-2230, 8am to 4pm, Monday through Friday or use the order form at the end of the book. Also see the catalog ad at the end of the book. **Our catalog is FREE with the purchase of any title listed, or $5.00 if sold separately.**

YOU WILL ALSO WANT TO READ:

☐ **76041 THE OUTLAW'S BIBLE,** *by E.X. Boozhie.* The best "jailhouse" law book ever published — for people on the outside who want to stay there. This is a real life civics lesson for citizen lawbreakers: how to dance on the fine line between freedom and incarceration, how to tiptoe the tightrope of due process. Covers detention, interrogation, searches and seizures. The only non-violent weapon available for those on the wrong side of the law. *1985, 5½ x 8½, 336 pp, index, soft cover.* **$16.95**

☐ **91095 FREE SPACE! Real Alternatives for Reaching Outer Space,** *by B. Alexander Howerton.* The author is the editor of *Space Available*, a newsletter for investors in space-related stocks. He delivers an explosive critique of NASA, then describes the efforts of ten successful companies that will open outer space to commercial travel in the next decade. Covers builders of rockets, shuttles, rovers, space stations, and modular human habitats for the Moon, Mars and beyond. Contains rare photos and illustrations. *1995, 5½ x 8½, 152 pp, illustrated, soft cover.* **$14.95**

☐ **94146 LOOMPANICS' GREATEST HITS, Articles and Features from the Best Book Catalog in the World,** *Edited by Michael Hoy.* A collection of articles and essays, cartoons and rants, gleaned from the pages of the Loompanics Unlimited book catalog. For over a decade, the Loompanics Catalog has served as a kiosk for writers from the far left, the far right and the *far out* — including Robert Anton Wilson, Bob Black, Kurt Saxon, Robert Shea and many, many others. A compendium of counterculture thought, this provocative book contains more than 75 features in all. *1990, 8½ x 11, 308 pp, illustrated, soft cover.* **$14.95**

To order any of the above titles or titles on the following pages by credit card, call 1-800-380-2230, 8am to 4pm, Monday through Friday or use the order form at the end of the book. Also see the catalog ad at the end of the book. **Our catalog is FREE with the purchase of any title listed, or $5.00 if sold separately.**

YOU WILL ALSO WANT TO READ:

☐ **94207 LOOMPANICS' GOLDEN RECORDS, Articles and Features from The Best Book Catalog in the World,** *Edited by Michael Hoy.* This brand new collection contains more than 40 of the best and most imaginative pieces Loompanics has ever published, including work by Bob Black, Jim Hogshire, Michael Newton, James B. DeKorne, and many others. *Loompanics' Golden Records* also features artwork by some of America's most talented artists, such as Mark Zingarelli, Nick Bougas, and Ace Backwords. *1993, 8½ x 11, 200 pp, illustrated, soft cover.* **$10.95**

☐ **94268 LOOMPANICS UNLIMITED LIVE! IN LAS VEGAS,** *Edited by Michael Hoy.* Every three years or so, Loompanics Unlimited lights up the desert landscape of American letters by compiling a collection of articles and stories, culled from the catalogs and supplements that we've published during that time. Since we've specialized in providing controversial and unusual works for over twenty years, it should come as no surprise to anyone that many of the selections in this book are both shocking and exhilarating. *1996, 8½ x 11, 255 pp, illustrated, soft cover.* **$14.95**

☐ **25081 VEST-BUSTERS: How To Make Your Own Body-Armor-Piercing Bullet,** *by Uncle Fester.* What do you do when you're attacked by armed invaders who are wearing Kevlar body armor? If you've followed this book's clear, concise instructions, you're ready to drop them in their tracks! That's because it explains how to select and modify the most effective kinds of bullets, procure the necessary coating materials without arousing any suspicion, and efficiently apply a Teflon coating that will enable the concerned home defender to confront and defeat any and all intruders who have clad themselves in Kevlar body armor! Don't be a victim... be a victor instead! Give yourself the winning edge, and learn how to make your own body-armor-piercing bullets! *Sold for informational purposes only. 1996, 5½ x 8½, pp, illustrated, soft cover.* **$12.00**

To order any of the above titles or titles on the following pages 72 by credit card, call 1-800-380-2230, 8am to 4pm, Monday through Friday or use the order form at the end of the book. Also see the catalog ad at the end of the book. **Our catalog is FREE with the purchase of any title listed, or $5.00 if sold separately.**

ORDER FORM

- ☐ 85225 A Man's Guide To Advertising For A Woman, $16.95
- ☐ 25065 Armed Defense, $16.95
- ☐ 14099 Art & Science Of Dumpster Diving, $14.95
- ☐ 55090 Be Your Own Dick, $12.00
- ☐ 10048 Big Book Of Secret Hiding Places, $14.95
- ☐ 14177 Community Technology, $9.95
- ☐ 32060 David's Tool Kit, $16.95
- ☐ 14181 Eat Well For 99¢ A Meal, $14.95
- ☐ 91095 Free Space!, $14.95
- ☐ 17056 Freedom Road, $16.95
- ☐ 13068 Getting Started In The Underground Economy, $14.95
- ☐ 13044 Guerrilla Capitalism, $14.95
- ☐ 25052 Homemade Guns And Homemade Ammo, $14.95
- ☐ 14185 How To Build Your Own Log Home For Less Than $15,000, $19.95
- ☐ 10049 How To Bury Your Goods, $8.00
- ☐ 17054 How To Buy Land Cheap, $14.95
- ☐ 76059 How To Clear Your Adult And Juvenile Criminal Records, $12.95
- ☐ 14176 How To Develop A Low-Cost Family Food-Storage System, $10.00
- ☐ 10065 How To Hide Things In Public Places, $15.00
- ☐ 61147 How To Legally Obtain A Second Citizenship And Passport, $15.00
- ☐ 17028 How To Start Your Own Country, $12.95
- ☐ 17084 I Walked Away, $14.95
- ☐ 94207 Loompanics' Golden Records, $10.95
- ☐ 94146 Loompanics' Greatest Hits, $14.95
- ☐ 94268 Loompanics Unlimited Live! In Las Vegas, $14.95
- ☐ 94101 Natural Law, $7.95
- ☐ 14183 The 99¢ A Meal Cookbook, $14.95
- ☐ 10060 Our Vanishing Privacy, $12.95
- ☐ 76041 Outlaw's Bible, $16.95
- ☐ 19188 Personal Defense Weapons, $12.00
- ☐ 70050 Pirate Radio Operations, $19.95
- ☐ 85212 The Politics Of Consciousness, $18.95
- ☐ 58080 The Privacy Poachers, $16.95
- ☐ 91085 Secrets Of A Super Hacker, $19.95
- ☐ 14175 Self-Sufficiency Gardening, $13.95
- ☐ 55052 Shadowing And Surveillance, $16.95
- ☐ 19197 Street Smarts For The New Millennium, $15.00
- ☐ 17079 Travel-Trailer Homesteading Under $5,000, $8.00
- ☐ 25081 Vest-Busters, $12.00
- ☐ 17025 Vonu, $10.00
- ☐ 14178 Wild And Free Cookbook, $19.95
- ☐ 40083 You Are Going To Prison, $14.95
- ☐ 88888 1997 Loompanics Unlimited Main Catalog, $5.00

Loompanics Unlimited
PO Box 1197
Port Townsend, WA 98368

REVO98

Please send me the books I have checked above. I have enclosed $_____ which includes $4.95 for the shipping and handling of the first $20.00 ordered. Add an additional $1 shipping for each additional $20 ordered. Washington residents include 7.9% sales tax.

Name_____

Address _____

City/State/Zip _____

VISA and MasterCard accepted. 1-800-380-2230 for credit card orders *only*.
8am to 4pm, PST, Monday through Friday.